D1221673

SUCCESS
with PEOPLE

SUCCESS
with PEOPLE

Instant Solutions for Your Toughest Problems at Work and at Home

JAMES K. VAN FLEET

BARNES
&NOBLE
BOOKS
NEW YORK

To my beloved wife, Belva Van Fleet, who has been a source of inspiration to her entire family, because of her courage, her patience, and her cheerful optimism, in spite of her many years of painful suffering with an incurable physical condition.

Originally published as *Lifetime Guide to Success With People*

Copyright © 1995 by James K. Van Fleet

This edition is reprinted in hardcover by Barnes & Noble, Inc., by arrangement with Prentice-Hall Direct, a division of Pearson Education

2001 Barnes & Noble Books

ISBN 0-7607-2389-3

Printed and bound in the United States of America

01 02 03 04 MC 9 8 7 6 5 4 3 2 1

MRT

WHAT THIS BOOK WILL DO FOR YOU

Most self-improvement and "how-to" books require readers to get through twenty to twenty-five pages per chapter before they come across the answer to their specific problem. I, too, have become discouraged in reading someone else's self-help book when I have had to read a great many pages before finding the answer I needed.

So I decided to do things differently in this book. Instead of old-style chapters, I have divided the book into "problems." I have broken down each broad problem into bite-sized *solutions* to specific questions. This way, you will be able to find the answer you need quickly and easily. Each solution in this book will have on the average two to three pages—at the most, six or seven pages. I know you will enjoy this new easy to use format.

The book is divided into three major parts. Each part contains major sections that have short chapters. Part One covers Instant Solutions to On-the-Job-Problems. Because most of the problems in your relationships with people occur in the workplace, the majority of this book will be devoted to that subject. Part One, then, contains the following sections:

Problem #1: Getting on the Right Track at Work. You'll be shown how to stay out of trouble on your job, how to keep your job from getting you down, and how to assess your own performance.

Problem #2: Gaining Control of Your Job. Here you'll learn how to manage your time successfully, how to keep from wasting time, how to ask your subordinates for their advice, and how to give them your cooperation first to get theirs.

Problem #3: Navigating the Organizational Waters. The areas discussed here include how to get the raise you're entitled to, how to get ahead in a big company, how to sell your ideas to your boss, how to develop a positive personal image, how to handle the individual who tries to use "borrowed power" to get ahead, how to develop a cordial relationship with your colleagues, how to read the company's "invisible" power chart, and how to use office politics properly to get ahead.

Problem #4: Becoming a Better Boss. You'll learn how to avoid many of the problems bosses create for themselves, why you should always tell the truth, why trying to be liked instead of respected is a mistake, how to set a personal example for others to follow, and why you should not use your position for personal gain at the expense of others.

Problem #5: Making Yourself Into a Leader. This section discusses the traits of leadership you need to develop, how to control large groups of people, how to find the key people in any group, how to handle the problem person, and how to make sound and timely decisions.

Problem #6: Developing Workplace Guidelines. Here you'll learn the importance of emphasizing skills, not rules, how to use an SOP to prevent problems from happening, and the importance of completed staff work.

Problem #7: Solving Supervisory Problems. You'll learn the proper way to correct a subordinate's mistakes, how to solve employee gripes, how to ask the right questions, and how to handle an angry employee.

Problem #8: Communicating with Your Employees. Here you'll learn how you can use body language, how to read another person's body language, how to keep your employees informed and up to date, and how to ensure that they will let you know what's going on in your organization.

Problem #9: Motivating Employees. You'll discover how to make your people part of the team, how to use competition to get maximum results, how to build a superior outfit with ordinary people, how to make every employee superior, and how to use the "buffer technique" to get results.

Problem #10: Improving Overall Productivity. You'll learn how to take responsibility for your actions, how to get your subordinates to accept responsibility, how to make sure the job is understood, how to properly inspect your subordinates' work, how to go for the maximum, how to control your emotions on the job, and how to treat your subordinates as individuals.

Problem #11: Succeeding in Your Own Business will tell you how to let your business do your talking for you, how to use twenty-four tips to succeed, and why your attitude can spell the difference between success and failure.

Problem #12: Mastering Sales Techniques will give you the techniques you can use to write a persuasive sales letter, how to gain immediate attention and hold it, how to overcome resistance, the three secrets of super salespeople, how to sell the right person on your product or service, and how to find out what a person wants.

Problem #13: Presenting Yourself in the Best Light. Here you'll learn how to speak in a meeting, how to conduct a meeting, how to speak at employees' affairs, how to give a VIP briefing, and how to build important community contacts for yourself.

Problem #14: Winning Strategies for Women provides advice specifically geared to women: how to be successful in a man's world, how to develop the aura of power, how a secretary climbed her way to success in a big company, and how you can succeed in your own business.

Part Two gives you Instant Solutions to Problems Outside the Workplace, for example, situations that can arise with your neighbors, friends, and social acquaintances. Although Part Two is shorter than Part One, it should not be considered less important. In fact, many of the problems and situations covered in Part One can also occur with your friends, neighbors, and social acquaintances and solutions can be modified to fill those needs.

Problem #15: Connecting with People will show you how to overcome shyness, how to be the center of attention, how not to become a loner, how to win friends, and how to combine friendship and business.

Problem #16: Making Friends, Not Enemies gives you the techniques you can use to avoid making enemies, how to turn an enemy into a friend, how to turn off a person's anger immediately, and a six-step technique for winning every argument.

Problem #17: Dealing with Strangers will show you how to strike up a conversation with a complete stranger, how to get a complete stranger to go out of his way to help you, three sure-fire ways to make friends with a stranger, and how to talk to a woman and vice versa.

Part Three is devoted to Instant Solutions to Family Problems. Although not so large as Part One, the information it contains will be a big help to you.

Problem #18: Creating a Happier Home Life will show you how to use participatory management in the home, how to get your family to do as you ask, how to guide your children without effort, how to create a friendly family atmosphere, and how a family "love feast" will quickly solve your marital problems.

Problem #19: Making Your Marriage Work will give you a technique that will literally work magic for you with your spouse, will help a wife to help her husband succeed at his job, and provide techniques to use if you're newly married.

Before we move into the text, I want to share this insight gained in more than thirty years as a consultant in business management and human relations: Success depends as much on a person's ability to get along with others as it does on professional and technical skills.

This book will give you the strategies you need to succeed in your dealings with other people in any and all circumstances. You'll be given instant solutions for problems you encounter or difficult situations in which you find yourself. You'll also be shown how to influence and control specific key individuals in your life by what you say and do so you can achieve your goals and become highly successful.

When you learn how to deal successfully with people, you'll be at home in any social environment. You can walk into any group and be as much at ease as if you were with your own friends or family. On the job, you'll know what to do and say with your boss, your co-workers, and your employees in order to achieve the greatest success. Outside the workplace, you'll find that friends, neighbors, strangers, and even enemies will do what you want. In fact, wherever you go, you'll be nailed as a leader; you'll be treated with dignity and respect; people will listen to you and do as you want them to do. At home, you'll create harmony and gain cooperation from your loved ones.

Lifetime Guide to Success with People is an organized, cohesive, and sure-fire program for getting ahead and gaining both your social and professional goals. And it will continue to help you succeed and grow throughout the rest of your life.

After you've finished reading your *Lifetime Guide to Success with People* for the first time, you will want to refer to it again and again to find the instant solution for every situation you encounter and the answer to every people problem you have. All you need do is turn to the appropriate problem to find your answer.

If you will use your *Lifetime Guide to Success with People* as a ready reference book, you'll never be at a loss as to what to do or say, for you'll be able to find the instant solution for every situation you encounter and the answer to every problem you need to solve.

Now on to the first problem in Part One: Getting on the Right Track at Work. I sincerely hope that you will enjoy reading my book as much as I have enjoyed writing it.

James K. Van Fleet

CONTENTS

Instant
Solutions
to
On-the-Job
Problems

Because most of the problems and difficult situations you will encounter in your relationships with people occur in the workplace, most of this book will be devoted to that subject.

GETTING ON THE RIGHT TRACK AT WORK

SOLUTIONS: STAY OUT OF TROUBLE; START OFF ON THE RIGHT FOOT

It's easier to stay on the right track than to get back on it once you're off. The best strategy for getting along with your new boss is to set the stage for a good relationship early in the game, says Orlando, Florida, management expert, Dale Wilson:

"First impressions are very hard to change. If you start out on the wrong foot with your employer, it can take a lot of work to overcome those negative impressions."

To get on the good side of your boss, Dale and other management consultants recommend using the following eight techniques:

1. ***Tone down your personality a bit when you're starting a new job.*** If you're too voluble and smooth-tongued, you could create the impression that you don't take your work seriously enough. It's much better to find out how the office runs and what the overall situation is rather than try to impress your co-workers with how much you know. You'll have plenty of time to loosen up after you've proved yourself to be dependable.

2. ***Don't put on a false front.*** When you do that, you'll soon tire of the pretense and your real personality will come through. When that happens, your boss could easily lose trust in you. If you think you have to stay constantly on guard to hold your job, it could be that the position is not for you.

"When your personality is totally in conflict with your job or your boss, you should move on because you'll never be completely happy with that job," says Patricia Fields. "And I speak from personal experience: Several years ago, I left a good paying sales job because the boss was too arbitrary about the way his salespeople were to act and how sales were to be made."

3. ***Don't talk about your previous job.*** Above all, don't compare your new job unfavorably with your old one. Saying to your supervisor "That isn't the way I did it at my old job" won't win her approval; she couldn't care less about how you did it before.

4. ***Don't make critical remarks about your new job.*** It's better not to question the status quo until you have a better understanding and knowledge about how the organization ticks. If and when you do approach your boss to make a suggestion, word it in such a way that it isn't insulting. Be careful not to appear to be uncooperative or a know-it-all.

5. ***Learn what your boss's personal style is.*** Is she a no-nonsense, facts and figures person? Does she like to share personal experiences?

Your fellow employees can give you an insight into your boss's personality, but don't be misled by their subjective opinions. You must be objective and learn to speak the same language.

Tom Watson, a university psychologist in Atlanta, Georgia, says, "You can't control another person's personality. You can only control how you react to it," which is excellent advice for all occasions, but especially when relating to your boss.

6. ***In the beginning, be willing to put in more hours.*** Work a little harder to speed up the learning process. Work some extra hours and take some reading material home.

"However, if you want your new boss to know that you're really motivated, don't do all that extra work at home," says Teresa Jackson, a computer programmer with a large electronics company in Palm Bay, Florida. "It's far better if you do a lot of that extra work and reading in the office where your boss can see you staying late to learn your new job."

7. *Get a clear mental picture of exactly what your boss expects of you.* If you want to have a good relationship with your boss, you must know what your exact duties are and what is expected of you. A conference early on can head off trouble.

8. *Admit mistakes immediately.* If you make a mistake, and you will, admit it immediately. Don't try to cover it up or pass the buck. Accept the responsibility at once.

A small mistake that is covered up can turn into a nightmare and completely destroy your superior's confidence in you. When you make a mistake, talk it over with your boss so you can find out where you went wrong and how you can avoid making that same mistake in the future.

SOLUTIONS: EIGHT WAYS TO GET BACK ON TRACK

One of the biggest headaches your job can give you is getting on the wrong track with your boss. Whether you're at fault or your boss is really doesn't matter. The first action you need to take is to get back on track.

Getting on your boss's bad side may be temporary or it may sidetrack or even ruin your career with that company. No matter what the ultimate effect, the experience can be upsetting and nerve wracking.

For example, Gregory Stewart, a junior executive with a large Miami, Florida, investment company, lashed out at his superior just a few days before he was up for promotion:

"I went home realizing that I'd risked a sure-fire promotion by arguing with my superior over a decision that wasn't even mine to make! I felt the most important thing for me to do was to apologize to my boss and tell him I was way out of line." The end result? He got the promotion he deserved.

If you've too much time invested in the company to quit and go elsewhere, here are eight techniques you can use to get back in your boss's good graces.

1. *Recognize your own shortcomings.* Before you consult with anyone, take an inventory of yourself. Figure out if the problem is you, your boss, or a combination.

"You might be in the doghouse because your superior is unreasonable or biased, which might have nothing at all to do with your actual work on the job," says Rodney Charles, a professor of organizational behavior at a Florida university.

"Or it could be that your communicating with other people in the company causes him to believe you're talking about him behind his back. Whatever the cause, figure out what the problem is and solve it so you can get back on his good side as soon as possible."

2. *Determine whether something is bothering you, then fix it.* It might be as simple a thing as changing your outlook or your attitude.

A Des Moines, Iowa, management consultant for a conservative public relations firm once got into trouble for being late to work and for wearing casual attire. What was his problem? "I wanted to show them how unhappy and dissatisfied I was with their conservative approach," Malcolm said.

"I finally realized the problem was my attitude, not theirs. When I decided to change it, it dramatically changed my outlook and helped me to be promoted."

3. *Talk frankly and openly with your boss.* Find out what your boss thinks about you and whether he or she is willing to work with you.

"Employees can do much to help themselves by being up front with the boss," Gerald Myer, now an employer rather than an employee, says. "As a boss dealing with employees, I respect someone who says to me, 'I did this wrong and I'm going to work on correcting my mistake.'"

4. *Have a plan for improvement.* "Give your boss a well-thought-out plan for how you can do a better job for him," Carol Barnes, a legal secretary, says. "Get suggestions on how to do that from your friends and colleagues, who will help you move your career ahead. Make sure your plan has goals, timetables, and periodic reviews."

5. *Ask your boss to tell you how you can improve your performance.* This will help you keep the discussion focused on your job performance and away from any personality clash.

But don't settle for broad vague statements like a high school shop teacher used when he told my son, Larry, "Oh, that's all wrong!" on a project he was working on. Ask for examples of mistakes you've made and specific ways you could have handled things differently.

6. *Update or change your skills.* Sometimes a person can be in trouble with the boss because he no longer has the skills to handle more challenging assignments. For example, some people are afraid to learn computer skills or other new tasks necessary to get ahead in today's job market.

7. *Request a transfer.* Short of leaving the company, you might be able to move to another department or section. Learn some new skills that will help you get to a new department or different division in your company if the differences between you and your boss seem irreconcilable.

8. *If none of the previous techniques work, leave.* If you've tried in vain to get back into your boss's good graces but failed, it might be best to look for a new job in a different company. Before you make that decision, however, here are four final tips to help you get out of the rut you're in:

- ✔ *Don't* complain to anyone who will listen. *Do* talk to only one person about your problem. Ask for advice from a colleague whom you trust and admire. Be honest. Recognize your own shortcomings; don't blame all your problems on your superiors.

- ✔ *Don't* stew or sulk. *Do* get something done, even when you're sulking. Answer memos, go through your mail. Empty your in-box. Keep it simple.

- ✔ *Don't* show up late for meetings. *Do* be on time. Improve your personal planning to get more organized.

- ✔ *Don't* retreat from your job and your co-workers. *Do* mingle. Eat lunch with your co-workers to keep your work ties and stay connected with issues in the company.

SOLUTIONS: A DO-IT-YOURSELF PERFORMANCE APPRAISAL

I've never been able to appraise my own job performance honestly using one of those forms with blocks or squares in which to put check marks.

I have, however, developed a set of eight simple questions that have been much more useful in honestly assessing my own job performance. All of them except the first one can be answered with one word—yes or no. And I could quickly tell whether or not I was doing the job I was being paid to do. Here are the questions:

1. **_Do you give your boss problems or solutions?_** You have enough problems of your own to solve without having your subordinates bring their problems to you to take care of, right? Your boss feels the same way. This is not to say that you shouldn't turn to your superior for help when you need it, but you should not bring her only your problems. Bring her a couple of tentative solutions too.

"I keep my eye on an employee who brings me a proposed solution or two with his problem," says Alfred Stone, executive vice president of a business machines manufacturing company in Chicago. "Chances are he's a comer, a doer, as well as a thinker, and I earmark him for promotion over those who bring me their problems with no possible solutions."

So the next time you take a problem to your boss, take along some possible answers, too. It's the best way to present yourself as a comer, a doer, and a thinker.

2. **_Do you try to get all the facts before you respond?_** "Sometimes it's a mistake to be first with an answer unless you know for sure it's the right answer. Speed doesn't always indicate accuracy," says Ellen Newman, chief of the laboratory section of a large California hospital. "I know we can't waste time, for many doctors are waiting for our reports so they can know how to proceed in treating their patients, but unless our reports are accurate, they're worse than useless. The lives of the patients can depend on us."

Without a doubt, the least glamorous part of any job is the minutiae—the endless and monotonous details. But before you start giving your boss answers, gather enough details to make sure your answer is correct.

3. *When you're given an assignment, do you use all available resources to get the job done?* Perhaps you've been asking questions and getting answers like these: "You can find the answer to your question in the file on that subject. . . . I sent out a memo to all departments explaining that point last week. . . . Go over your notes from yesterday's meeting; I discussed that point in complete detail then." Chances are you're not using your head or all your resources to get the job done.

If you rarely go to your boss with questions and know his thinking and viewpoint before you start, you're doing the right thing. And he'll think so too.

4. *Do your reports stick to the point and present only the results?* Production reports, sales reports, construction reports, and the like should tell what you've actually done, the results you've obtained. Your boss isn't interested in how much trouble you've had in getting the job done unless you've wasted company resources. She's interested only in results and that's all your report should contain, nothing more.

Reports are essential, of course. But a long, involved, detailed report is often a substitute for action. The person who gets the job done usually says little but does much.

5. *Do you meet deadlines?* Rare is the manager who can get the job done without watching the clock and the calendar. *When* something is done is often just as important as *what* is done.

"I can't use a person who doesn't get her work done on time," says Sylvia Thompson, controller and financial director of a large Iowa radio corporation. "No matter how complete and accurate the work might be, if I can't depend on the person to get it done on time, I just can't use that individual in our company."

If you're going to meet deadlines, never take your eye off the target date. If unforeseen problems come up, let your superior know right away so the due date can be reviewed and perhaps changed. Don't wait until deadline day and then say you couldn't get your work done or the report done.

6. *Do you finish the job you start?* Starting a job is a lot easier than finishing it. The early phases of thinking about a new project, getting your ideas down on paper, talking to your associates

about it are exciting. But as that first flush of excitement fades away, tedious details and problems creep in.

To ensure that you do finish each job you start, you'll need persistence. President Calvin Coolidge once said: "Nothing in the world can take the place of persistence. Talent will not; nothing is more common than unsuccessful men with talent. Genius will not; the world is full of educated derelicts. Persistence and determination are omnipotent. The slogan 'Press on!' has solved and always will solve the problems of the human race."

If you have that kind of persistence, you'll finish *every* job you start.

7. ***Do you try to slough off the details?*** If you really want to get the job done, you won't run away from the details. I've had would-be writers come up to me after one of my seminars and say, "Tell me now, you don't really have to worry much about your punctuation, grammar, spelling, that sort of thing when you write, do you? I mean if you really have something worthwhile to say, the editor will take care of those minor details, won't he?"

My answer to that is always quite blunt. "No, he won't!" If you're careless about those *minor* details of punctuation, spelling, grammar, and word usage, your editor can legitimately suspect that you're careless about your facts, too. Besides, that's your job, not your editor's job.

8. ***Do you panic easily?*** It's easy enough to work and get a job done when things are going smoothly and there are no problems. Anyone can do that. But the rough days, when you are confronted with obstacles and problems, are the real testing ground.

If you can remain calm and keep your cool under conditions that would cause the average person to lose it, you'll be worthy of additional responsibility and promotion. You'll be getting things done while others around you are running for cover.

If you answered the first question with the word *solutions,* the second through the sixth with *yes,* and the last two with *no,* then you're a doer, not just a noisemaker. The finest reputation you can build with your boss is to have it said of you that *you get things done.* You'll become known as a *can-do person* who can be depended on to get the job done. Business and industry are always looking for such people. They are sought after for they are so few in number.

Use the eight questions to assess your own performance honestly and realistically, and you can be one of those can-do people, too.

Gaining Control of Your Job

SOLUTIONS: MANAGE YOUR TIME BY MANAGING YOURSELF

Many managers and executives work sixty and more hours every week, including at least ten hours outside the office. Some of them use not only their lunch hours to conduct business and solve problems, but also their dinner hours as well. At the end of an already overly long day, they carry home briefcases full of even more work to be done during their "leisure" time, when they should be free to be with their families or enjoy some relaxing pastime with their friends. Do you fit in this category? If you do, then this chapter is a must for you.

The end result of all this frenzied activity can be what is called *hurry sickness*. Hurry sickness, also known as the stress syndrome, causes an excessive amount of adrenaline to be pumped into your vascular system. Your heart beats faster, the lungs work harder, and you tire more quickly.

This kind of stress can lead to duodenal ulcers, high blood pressure, heart attacks, headache, low back pain, diarrhea, asthma and eczema, as well as a long list of other physical and psychological problems. These conditions are usually known as *Emotionally Induced Illness*. Too much time spent on the job is also one of the leading causes of marital conflict and divorce.

The fourteen leading wasters of time on the job are these:

1. Telephone interruptions

2. Unscheduled and unwanted visitors

3. Meetings, both routine and special

4. Unplanned situations

5. No management goals and objectives

6. Cluttered desk, stacked up paperwork, and personal disorganization

7. Inability to concentrate fully

8. Trying to do too many things at once

9. Doing work that should be delegated to others

10. No clear lines of authority and responsibility

11. Personal indecision and procrastination

12. Inaccurate or untimely information from others

13. No clear and concise instructions

14. Inability to say "No!" and stick to it

When you review this list carefully, you'll notice that in not one case is the actual management of time the basic problem. The real problem is the management of one's self. Training and self-discipline will eliminate these fourteen time wasters. Here's how to do that:

Watching the clock will not break your bad habits of procrastinating and wasting time; only self-discipline will do that. Once you understand and accept the basic premise that you, not the clock, are the master of time, then everything else will fall naturally into its proper place. Then the management of time will become easy for you.

When you stop watching the clock, you'll learn to concentrate fully on the job at hand. Of all the principles of time management, none is more important than the amount of *uninterrupted time* that's spent on the job.

This idea of not watching the clock but watching yourself and your activities to manage time is not unique to me. Other managers and executives have learned to use the same master key to control themselves and, therefore, to control their use of time. Carl J. Shelton, an executive vice-president with a large automobile manufacturer, is one such manager. Mr. Shelton says:

"I never really learned to manage my time so I could make the most of it until I learned to discipline and control myself, I believe my hardest job was forcing myself not to get involved in the details of the work that others should do. I had to drive myself to delegate every detail I possibly could to my subordinates. I eliminated all the unnecessary jobs I was doing and learned to manage my time by organizing and planning my work schedule. Managing and disciplining myself was the only way I was ever able to manage and control my time."

Forcing yourself to delegate work to your subordinates may not be the problem for you that it was for Mr. Shelton. Another of those other fourteen time wasters that I just gave you may be your major problem. Just determine where your major problem is and correct it.

Remember that the master key to your use of time is learning to manage yourself. When you learn how to control, train, manage, and discipline yourself, as well as your subordinates, then these fourteen leading wasters of time will no longer be a problem.

SOLUTIONS: DON'T WASTE YOUR TIME ON OTHER PEOPLE'S WORK

As I mentioned earlier, the hardest job Carl J. Shelton had was keeping himself from getting involved in the work of his subordinates.

Not only is getting involved in the details of your subordinates' work a waste of your time, but it also is one of the quickest ways to lower their morale.

"To delegate authority to your subordinates for the details of the work that is to be done is a sign of good management," says Linda Roland, a supervisor in a large computer supply company in Atlanta, Georgia. "If you insist on keeping your hand in the details of their work all the time, you'll discourage your subordinates by competing with them. And then, the capable ones will leave you. The lazy ones will sit back and let you do all the work for them. In the end, you'll have no time left for your own job as a leader and a manager: thinking, planning, organizing, controlling."

No manager, no matter how competent, can do everything by herself nor should she try. A wise executive can expand her influence and her ability to serve her organization only through the art of delegating the work to be done.

If you try to do it all yourself, you'll have to, for you'll be the only one left to do it. As the president of one large company so succinctly told his personnel manager, "Find the person we can't get along without and then fire him! I'm scared to death of him if he's indispensable. What would we do if he suddenly died? He would leave us incapable of doing our work and getting the job done!"

If you cannot delegate the details to your subordinates, you are no manager. You are an overworked, underpaid, one-person army. You will end up being the hardest working person in the organization and also the least efficient. If you cannot bring yourself to let your subordinates do their work, you'll soon be smothered in a mass of details yourself.

"Fear causes a lot of managers to hang on to the details of the work that belongs to their subordinates to do," says Wendall Garrison, a foreman in charge of production in a large cleaning products company in New Jersey.

"They're afraid that if they allow their subordinates to carry out the details of their work and make their own decisions to do that, something will happen that could seriously endanger their own position. They imagine all sorts of problems and troubles that could come up if they surrender any part of their authority to their subordinates."

The kind of manager Wendall is talking about is quite common. To tell the truth, most of us feel we could do the job better than anyone else. Many managers look at delegation of authority to do the details of the work as a loss of control. But it doesn't have to be that way at all.

The smart manager will delegate both the authority and the responsibility *only after he has established the proper control measures that will allow him to take immediate action if something does go wrong.* Those control measures are

1. Your subordinates must first be thoroughly trained, qualified, and capable of doing the job.
2. They should be assigned their responsibilities, in a systematic way, one step at a time, not all at once.
3. You should correct their mistakes and praise their successes as they carry out their assignments and responsibilities.
4. At each critical point, have your controls set up in such a way that you can move in at once to stop or take over anything that might seriously jeopardize successful completion of the job or that would endanger your position or your employee's position.

Remember that delegating the responsibility and the authority for the details of the work to be done builds a feeling of self-confidence in your staff. It's definite proof that you have faith in them and in their abilities. You'll also gain their respect and develop their initiative and resourcefulness.

To sum up: About two thousand years ago, Horace, the famous Roman poet, said, "I mind the business of other people, having lost my own!" If you follow the four simple guidelines I've just given you, you won't find yourself in that position.

SOLUTIONS: ASK YOUR STAFF FOR THEIR ADVICE AND HELP

Not only should you delegate to your staff the authority to do the job without your interference, but you should also ask them for their advice and help. Remember that the person who's actually doing the job knows more about it than anyone else.

When you do ask your staff for their advice and help, you'll gain four specific benefits:

1. Your staff will feel they're part of the team.
2. You can identify those of above-average ability.
3. You'll give your employees a sense of importance.
4. They'll put their imagination, initiative, and ingenuity to work for you.

One of the best ways to gain these benefits is to *make subordinates feel that your problem is their problem.* All of us are more interested in our own problems than we are in someone else's. And your subordinates are more interested in their problems than they are in yours. So if you want to get your people interested in your problem, then you must make it theirs. I learned that technique from Harry Simpson, manager of a discount store in Springfield, Missouri, who said,

"One of the toughest problems I had to solve when I took over the management of this store was getting my department heads to cut costs and overhead and increase net profits. This store was showing the least profit of all the discount centers in the Midwest, and the owners wanted some definite corrective action taken to change that.

"Now the previous manager told me he'd tried preaching, sermonizing, pleading, appealing to loyalty, but with no results. So when I took over, I didn't try any of these methods. I didn't preach, scold, or try to persuade.

"I just assembled everyone and told them that unless we could cut costs and start showing a profit *this store was going to be closed and we'd all be out of a job! That one statement made my problem their problem immediately.*

"I gave each department head the responsibility for reducing the costs in his own area. I told them to get ideas from their own people and that we would reward each person whose idea was used.

"Before long I was flooded with all sorts of suggestions on how to save money on utilities, warehousing and storage costs, customer delivery service, packaging and shipping, even postage and telephone charges.

"Within six months we had reduced our operating costs by thirty-five percent and the store was showing an acceptable profit. And all because I made my problem their problem when I told them we'd all be out of a job if we didn't succeed in doing that."

You can use this same technique of making your problem your employees' problem. Set up your own employee think tank and give them your headaches to solve. Whatever you do and however you do it, remember that *the fastest way to solve your problem is to make it their problem, too.* And be sure to reward them when they do solve it for you.

You should also make it easy for your staff to communicate their ideas to you. In my own experience, I've found that the most effective way to get my subordinates to submit their ideas to me was not to use a suggestion box but to sit down with them and let them tell me about it verbally, face to face, one on one.

I did not sit behind my desk when I did that, which would have put them at a disadvantage. I sat down with them in my office at a coffee table where we could meet each other as equals and talk over their ideas without having that boss-employee relationship.

I always brought in some coffee, too. Then I told my secretary to see that we were not disturbed. I did everything I could to make them feel relaxed and comfortable so they could concentrate on the idea—not on office protocol.

After I listened to the suggestion, I said I would get to work on it at once and that I would let the person know what was going on with the idea. I never kept the person in the dark. I always kept him or her informed about the progress of the suggestion.

Finally, I made sure to reward the person for the idea: a bonus, a raise, a promotion, a letter of appreciation, a certificate of achievement, whatever was appropriate.

So ask your staff for their advice and help. You'll gain lots of dividends. But don't take my word for it. Put the techniques I've given you to work and see the results for yourself.

SOLUTIONS: *GIVE* COOPERATION AND YOU WILL *GET* IT

Twenty years ago when I was writing the book *The 22 Biggest Mistakes Managers Make and How to Correct Them**, I was working on a problem similar to this one. I was having trouble, for the words just didn't seem to come right. So after several days of wasted effort, I called a friend of mine, Joe Ewing, the local Sears Roebuck store manager for his advice and help.

---

*James K. Van Fleet, *The 22 Biggest Mistakes Managers Make and How to Correct Them* (West Nyack, New York: Parker Publishing Company, 1973).

"How can you make sure you get cooperation from your employees, Joe?" I asked him. "What methods do you use in your store?"

"What is the title of your chapter, Jim?" Joe asked me.

"Getting Cooperation from Your Employees and Subordinates."

"You're taking the wrong approach, Jim," he said. "You're looking at it the wrong way. Most managers, executives, and businesspeople say the same thing. They all complain that they don't *get* enough cooperation *from* their employees. But why don't they? What's their real problem? Who's actually at fault—the managers or their employees?

"I can tell you right now the managers are at fault, Jim. And what's more, I can also tell you where they're making their basic mistake. I know, for I made that same mistake myself for many years before I realized what I was doing wrong.

"They're not *giving* any cooperation *to* their employees first. That's why they're not getting any cooperation in return. *You must always give before you can expect to get. When you do that, you always get back more than you give away.* Think of cooperation that way, Jim, and you won't have any trouble at all."

Of course, Joe was right; he always was. Once my thinking got straightened out, the ideas came like rain and the words began to flow. The information Joe gave me is just as important today as it was then. When you cooperate with your employees first, you'll gain these eight marvelous benefits:

1. Your staff will cooperate with you.

2. Your problem employees will cooperate, too.

3. They'll respect you and have confidence in you.

4. You'll gain their loyalty and support.

5. They'll work with initiative, ingenuity, and enthusiasm.

6. They'll work together as a team with high spirit and morale, with a definite purpose and direction toward a common goal.

7. You'll make them feel they belong where they are.

8. They'll work just as hard as you do to get the job done.

Here are some techniques you can use to gain these wonderful benefits:

Give them a chance to participate in management.

As Jimmy Durante always used to say, "Everybody wants to get into the act!" Your employees want to have a say in how things are run. You can make them feel it's *their* company, too, by letting them have a part in the planning, decision making, and the formulation of rules and regulations, policies and procedures. You can use many ways to let your employees participate in management to gain their cooperation. Here are some examples:

Give them the opportunity to help make the rules.

One of the problems with the traditional way rules are formulated and administered is that managers at the top always dictate what is right and wrong for rank-and-file workers at the bottom.

Top management in the average company arbitrarily sets the rules for employees to follow; so do department managers and section supervisors. But most people don't like to be told what to do or what not to do. After all, rules are restrictions on one's personal liberties, so we tend to resist rules or disobey them altogether.

One of the best ways you can cooperate with your employees is to let them work out the rules and regulations and submit them to you for approval. You'll find that average employees will be much tougher on themselves than you are. And since those rules are *their* rules, the ones *they* made up, they'll be much more likely to follow them than if they were yours alone.

Give your employees a chance to take part in decisions.

When the people in your company have a say in the decision-making process, they'll be much more likely to cooperate with you. If they agree with the decision, they'll look at it as their own and they'll back it to the hilt. If they don't agree, they'll still back it more strongly than they would've otherwise, simply because you gave them the courtesy of considering their point of view fully and fairly.

Hold weekly conferences with your staff.

People like to know what's going on. They like to be let in on things so they can see how their efforts relate to overall company goals and achievements. You might call your people together on Monday morning, for instance, for a short fifteen-minute meeting to discuss what's needed for the coming week.

This would be a good time to encourage reports on problems or work difficulties and to talk about new developments for the future. It would also be an appropriate time to pass out bouquets. And you could encourage your staff to voice their complaints and let them work the steam out of their systems just as long as you don't let it get out of hand.

Another excellent technique you can use to gain cooperation from your employees is to *offer them a profit-sharing plan.* This is not the same as a wage-incentive plan. Under a wage-incentive plan, the more a person produces, the more he earns as an individual. Under a profit-sharing plan, a person shares in the actual profits of the company. The more the company makes, the more *all* the employees make, so all the workers are eager to cooperate with management.

One of the pioneers of the profit-sharing plan has been the Lincoln Electric Company of Cleveland, Ohio. James F. Lincoln started it all when he was president of the company. He worked out a plan with his employees so all the workers could share in the profits.

Did profit sharing work for them? You can judge for yourself. Here are some of the results they obtained in the first ten years they used the plan:

✔ Annual volume of business increased six and one-half times.

✔ Production costs were cut in half in spite of rising inflation.

✔ Stockholders' dividends quadrupled.

✔ Average employee's wages went up over 400 percent!

✔ Employee turnover was reduced to nearly zero.

✔ There were no strikes or work slowdowns.

Lincoln Electric's record of industrial achievement has been so outstanding that CBS has featured them on its Sunday night prime-time program, *Sixty Minutes.*

Your employees will cooperate with you too if you give them your cooperation first.

NAVIGATING THE ORGANIZATIONAL WATERS

SOLUTIONS: HOW TO GET THE RAISE YOU DESERVE

If you're working for somebody else, especially in a big company or corporation, getting the raise you deserve requires certain techniques to gain your boss's attention.

I talked at length with a career management specialist, Tina Gilchrist, who teaches people how to get ahead and enjoy their jobs. Her clients include corporate vice presidents, managers, supervisors, executives, bankers, secretaries, and many others—all of whom pay her handsomely for her advice.

You're extremely fortunate because you're going to get the same information here for free. First of all, preparation for your raise begins long before you actually ask for it. Ms. Gilchrist says that there are seven vital steps to take to prepare for your raise:

1. ***Become the authority in your field.*** It is absolutely essential to know your business and to keep on knowing it. Progress is perpetual. If you don't keep up with current developments in your profession, you'll be passed over for promotion. But don't think for

a moment that you are indispensable. No one is. I have a cousin who retired from the air force as a two-star general. He thought the service would fold up without him, but to his surprise and dismay, it has continued to do quite well.

2. *Establish a cordial working relationship with your boss.* No executive, manager, or supervisor will go out of her way to give a raise or a promotion to a person she doesn't respect or like. The average boss likes people who praise her sincerely and make her feel important.

Smart employees appreciate their bosses and show them that appreciation. You can do that, too, without polishing the apple or using false flattery. Incidentally, the best way to praise a person is to compliment her for what she *does,* not for what she *is.* Praise the act, not the person.

3. *Learn to blow your own horn.* The idea that if you just do a good job, promotions and raises will come automatically is a myth. Doing good work alone is not how recognition comes. Your boss expects you to do good work without making mistakes. After all, that's what you're being paid for. Make yourself noticed and stand out from the pack by calling favorable attention to yourself.

Often your boss doesn't know how good you really are. Let him know about your successes, both large and small, without being obnoxious or overbearing about it—in the office, at a business lunch, at an office party or some other social function, or anywhere else.

It also helps for you to become well-known in your community, for this brings credit and recognition to your company. So don't be shy. Be willing to speak to church groups or civic clubs in your field of expertise when possible.

Do anything you can to keep your name uppermost in your superior's mind. This is precisely the way effective advertising works. As one executive told me, "The most important thing about advertising is repetition. It takes constant repetition to build a reputation. We don't care whether people remember exactly what we say *about* our product. We just want them to remember the *name* of it. That's enough."

Remember, then, it's your reputation that's being advertised when you blow your own horn. If other people think you're the best, you'll come out on top. You must project a winning reputation so others will believe it.

4. ***Don't hesitate to delegate work.*** When you're in management, don't hesitate to delegate work to your subordinates. Every time you let something go, you free yourself to accept additional responsibilities.

Top managers and executives always feel much more at ease when they know a competent person is available to take care of new assignments and new developments. Be smart; let them know that person is you.

5. ***Keep your superiors informed and up to date.*** Without breathing down their necks, let them know that your assignment is under control and proceeding on schedule. This shows you are a dependable person who's getting the job done.

6. ***Psych yourself up for the actual raise negotiation.*** This is not the time to become shy or sell yourself short. In our system, we equate value with cost. Your value to your company has a direct relationship to how much you're being paid.

Let your boss know the benefits he'll receive when he grants your raise. The biggest benefit he'll gain is retaining your valuable services.

But before you issue any ultimatums, be sure you have a concrete job offer somewhere else. As a wise man once said, "The biggest fool in the world is the person who quits one job before he has another."

7. ***How to time your request for a raise.*** I've found the best time to nail your boss for a raise is just after you've done a really outstanding job on a difficult assignment and he says that himself.

Praise for a job well done is much appreciated. It is one of the basic desires we all have, but the object of working is to make money. The more you make, the more important you feel, and the better you can live.

If your boss won't come across with a raise right after you've done an excellent job, it could be that he never will. So it might be time for you to move on to where your talents and efforts will be more appreciated, not only psychologically, but financially as well.

SOLUTIONS: HOW TO GET AHEAD IN THE BIG ORGANIZATION

Not everyone has the desire to start his or her own business venture, primarily because they do not want to assume personal risk for the sake of profit. Many people are quite happy and content to work in a big company or a large corporation, and they often become extremely successful in doing so. A great many benefits are to be gained by being employed in large organizations:

✔ Job security, including retirement benefits.

✔ Health insurance plans, including hospitalization.

✔ No personal risks: you don't risk the danger of failure or bankruptcy that you might in your own business venture.

✔ The possibility of a huge salary in the upper-management and executive levels, especially if you become the chief executive officer, president, or chairperson of the board.

✔ Stock options and other large bonuses. For instance, one CEO of a large corporation holds more than $200 million in stock options.

Here are the seven techniques you can use to get to the top in a big company or large corporation:

1. ***Never make an issue of small matters.*** Go along with minor or insignificant points when you can do so without causing damage either to yourself or your position. When you do have to make an issue of something, be sure that it is a major point. Then your objection will stand out and you'll be remembered and respected for your professional attitude and conduct.

2. ***State your objection calmly and courteously.*** When you do disagree with a major point, back up that disagreement with logic, reason, facts, and good judgment. Objections based on emotion or how you "feel" about something won't carry much weight. If the final decision goes against your recommendation, don't carry a chip on your shoulder. Do your level best to support the selected course of action of your superior. That's the mark of a professional and a team player.

3. *Develop the "golden touch" in human relationships.* The ability to get along with others is an absolute must if you want to get ahead in a big company. You cannot move up the executive ladder of success if you make an enemy out of everyone. In fact, knowing how to handle people is one of the hallmarks of executive leadership. If you can't get along well with your associates, if you are constantly involved in verbal warfare with someone, you'll eventually be let go, no matter what your professional qualifications and abilities are.

4. *Be enthusiastic about your job.* Don't expect to move up the management ladder if you don't really have your heart in your work. Your boss can tell, for your attitude will be reflected on your face and in your actions.

If you can't go to work smiling because you love your job, I feel deeply sorry for you. Either try to get enthusiastic about your work or change jobs before it's too late.

5. *Don't be afraid to take reasonable risks.* Top-level executives expect their subordinates to have the courage to make decisions and take reasonable risks. If you always play it safe and close to the belt, you'll never get ahead. Good prior planning on your part will prevent most major problems from happening and greatly reduce the risks for you.

6. *Look for more responsibility.* The person who ducks responsibility will never get to the top. Upper-level executives are always on the lookout for those who can accept more and more responsibility. The person who can is labeled as a "comer."

When you delegate a job to someone else to do, you're not passing the buck. Instead, you're freeing yourself to accept additional responsibility. Top management is always happy to find a competent individual who is available to take care of new and difficult projects. If you want to climb the management ladder and achieve success, be that person.

7. *Dream up your own technique for advancement.* Donna L. used one of the cleverest techniques I've ever heard about to climb the management ladder to success quickly. Shortly after Donna went to work for a large company, she realized that promotion was going to be a slow, tedious process. Then she had a brilliant flash of inspiration.

One of her college sorority friends had gone to work for an executive recruiting firm. She, too, was anxious to get ahead and succeed. Donna gave her boss's name to her friend, who was able to entice him away from the firm. Donna then moved into her boss's old slot. She used the same procedure several times to reach her current position in top-level management, leaving behind others with more seniority and experience.

You may not be able to make this same technique work for you, but you can use your creative imagination to dream up a technique of your own to get ahead in a big company or large corporation.

And when you do come up with something new, do me a favor and drop me a line to let me know about it so I can use it in my book. I'll mention your name and give you credit for your discovery.

SOLUTIONS: HOW TO SELL YOUR IDEAS TO YOUR BOSS

Successfully selling your boss on your idea depends not only upon the specific words you use, but also on the research and preparation you do. You must know *what* you're going to talk about and *how* you're going to present your ideas.

What you're going to talk about should follow these three specific guidelines:

- ✔ **You must know your subject** inside out, backward and forward, from top to bottom. Be prepared to give your boss your recommendations when she asks for them. Don't ask her to make your decisions for you. She has enough problems of her own to solve. She'll appreciate you much more if you'll take some of the load off her shoulders by making decisions that she can support.

- ✔ **Know all the details of your proposition,** so you can answer any possible questions your boss might ask, but don't drown him in details during your presentation. Give him only the basic points he needs to understand your idea unless he asks for more information. He will assume that you have all the details of your plan worked out. A sharp boss will check you on a few of them at least just to be sure you know what you're doing.

✔ *Make your presentation brief, coherent, complete, and salesworthy.* Save time for your boss by having your idea outlined in writing so she can review it later if she so desires. A written outline of your plan will also help her to present your idea to her superior for approval.

Here is how you can *physically* put your ideas across to your boss:

1. *You must know and understand your boss's personality* and have the intelligence and adaptability to go along with it. To be able to bring your boss in sync with your way of thinking is just as important as being capable in your job. This is not polishing the apple. It is using applied psychology, applied where it will do the most good for you—on your own boss.

2. *Pay your boss the respect and deference he is due* when putting your idea across to him. Even if you don't really care for him that much, his position alone entitles him to some respect. A senator may not like the President, but you can bet your boots he'll address him respectfully as "Mr. President." As they used to tell me when I was in the army years ago, "You salute the uniform, not the person wearing it."

3. *Adopt a "nothing sacred" attitude about your idea.* Don't act as if your idea is a God-given revelation, and, thus, immune from criticism. It must be able to stand on its own merits because it's a good idea, not just because it's your idea.

4. *Be courteous when presenting your idea.* Develop insight and understanding of your boss's problems. Consider her feelings when offering your idea to her.

5. *Let your boss set the mood for your presentation.* After all, he's the boss so you must be able to roll with the punches and adopt whatever attitude the occasion dictates; flexible or firm, friendly or aloof, humorous or serious. In short, you must be able to play it by ear.

SOLUTIONS: HOW TO PROJECT A BUSINESSLIKE PERSONAL IMAGE

You can use three techniques to subtly project a businesslike personal image that will leave a positive impression on the top-level executives and managers in your organization.

1. *Create your own "space bubble."* In companies and corporations the general rule of thumb is that the more powerful you become and the higher you go, the larger the area that you can call your own.

Low-ranked employees may work together in groups in one large room. The supervisor might have only a glassed-in cubicle from which to both see and be seen by subordinates.

A young executive may have a private, although small, office. As a member of the management team, even if you're a junior one, you should be entitled to that.

No matter how small your office is, you can expand your own physical space bubble by placing visitors' chairs against the wall farthest from your desk. Another person should never be able to *invade* or *encroach* upon your personal territory by putting his arms on your desk.

2. *What to do about names and titles.* Never refer to yourself by your first name. If you call someone on the phone, for example, don't say, "This is Joe down in accounting." Don't even say "This is Joe Horner in accounting." Instead, just say, "This is Horner." If you've been there for some time, people should already know you're in accounting and don't need to be told that.

The use of first names encourages too much familiarity. In executive and management levels, familiarity is an invasion of privacy. It punctures your psychological space bubble. Be courteous and polite, of course, but keep people at arm's length.

When answering the phone, don't use your title. Don't say "This is Mr. Horner, or Superintendent Horner, or Doctor, Major, Professor," or whatever. The implication is that you're not strong enough to stand on your own if you do that. Just say "Horner," or "Horner speaking." The implication here is everyone should know who you are without your telling them. When introducing yourself to someone, say, "I'm Horner," or "My name is Horner." Again, the idea is that everyone knows who you are.

If you are a woman, follow the same procedure. This places you on the same level as your male associates. Never refer to yourself as *Miss, Mrs.,* or *Ms.*

Why is all this so important to you? Because people who depend on titles are using *borrowed power* to get by on. They have no real personal power of their own. I'll explain borrowed power to you fully in the next solution.

3. *Eliminate certain words from your vocabulary.* The use of the words *Sir* and *Ma'am* automatically places other people above you. You can bring yourself up to their level immediately by eliminating these words from your vocabulary.

Many women object to the term "Ma'am," especially young women. The word is old-fashioned and out of date. When I was a boy, calling a lady "Ma'am" was considered to be polite. But, today even ladies in their seventies and eighties don't respond well to the term, for it seems to indicate age more than courtesy and respect.

The use of *sir* and *ma'am* also places you on a lower level than the other person. These words imply *submissiveness.* You can be courteous without being submissive. If your boss asks if you've completed a certain task, don't answer with "Yes, sir." Just say, "Yes, Mr. Jones, I have."

Don't reply with only *yes* or *no* when answering a question from your superior. It sounds too curt or insolent. Answer *yes* or *no* in a short sentence. If the person to whom you are speaking has a title, you can use that, too. For instance, you can say, "Yes, Doctor, I have," "No, Major, I have not."

SOLUTIONS: HOW TO HANDLE PEOPLE WHO USE "BORROWED POWER"

The person who uses "borrowed power" in trying to influence and direct the actions of others has no real personal power. Borrowed power is agency power. Even though a person can use agency power to advantage, the power does not come from that person.

For example, in the military, people who use borrowed power to get what they want will usually be generals' aides and wives of high-ranking staff officers. In business, it can be the boss's secretary, a brother-in-law, nephew, or some other relative.

You can easily identify people with agency or borrowed power this way. They have nothing to offer to get what they're after. They always try to get what they want without fulfilling another person's needs. Because they have no real personal power to achieve their goals, they have to use the position or status of others who do have the power. In short, they are parasites. They always try to get something for nothing, usually by using veiled threats.

Another trick that people with borrowed power will try is to issue an order they are not authorized to give. The recipient of such an order will attempt to carry it out and then end up in trouble when he does. This is often what the person with borrowed power wants to happen.

You can easily recognize whether or not an order is legitimate by what you hear. If you hear phrases like, "This is what the boss wants . . . this is what the boss asked for . . . this is what the general manager said to do," watch out. In the end, when something goes wrong, it will be only your word against his.

The best way to keep this from happening to you is to follow this simple rule: *Never take orders from anyone outside your command line of authority.* If your boss tells you to do it, then do it. If *his* boss tells you to do it, do it. But if you're in personnel and someone in purchasing or sales or engineering tells you to do it, forget it. Tell him to run it through proper command channels if he wants it done.

When you know from experience how people use borrowed power to gain their ends, you'll know how to defend yourself. Some people will foolishly defer to those with borrowed power, primarily because of their fear that they could lose their position or status if they don't.

Be courteous, of course, but refuse to do their bidding. As soon as you stand your ground, the person with borrowed power will leave you alone. Give in and you'll be under his or her thumb forever. Remember that when the present power structure changes, people with borrowed power will be the first to go. When their source of power disappears, so will they. And so might you, if you've been catering to them.

SOLUTIONS: HOW TO ESTABLISH A CORDIAL RELATIONSHIP WITH THE PERSON WHO HAS REAL POWER

It is far more productive to establish a cordial working relationship with the person who has the real power than with the one who uses agency or borrowed power. People with the real power are those who really count in the long run. They'll be around long after those with borrowed power are gone. To establish those cordial working relationships, follow the basic premise I've stressed before: *find out what the other person wants and needs so you can help him or her get it.*

1. *How you can find out what the other person needs.* Get a little black notebook and keep your eyes and ears open so you can gather and record information about those individuals who are important to you and your career. Use the basic needs and desires every normal person has as your guide in gathering useful information about the person. Here are those basic needs and desires:

✔ Financial success: money and all the things that money will buy

✔ Recognition of efforts, reassurance of worth

✔ Social or group approval, acceptance by one's peers

✔ Ego-gratification, a feeling of pride and importance

✔ The desire to win, the need to be first, to excel, to be the best

✔ A sense of roots, belonging somewhere—either to a place or to a group

✔ The opportunity for creative expression

✔ The accomplishment or achievement of something worthwhile

✔ New experiences

✔ A sense of personal power

✔ Good health; freedom from sickness and disease; physical comfort

✔ Liberty and freedom, privacy from intrusion

✔ A sense of self-respect, dignity, and self-esteem

✔ Love in all its forms

✔ Emotional security

I have not listed these basic needs and desires in any particular order of importance, except for emotional security. It is listed last because if any one of the others is not fulfilled in a person's life, then it is impossible for that person to achieve emotional security.

If you don't remember anything else about human nature, keep these basic desires in mind, remembering that everything a person does is directed toward their fulfillment. Every thought, word, and deed is aimed at gaining these goals. Help them gain them and they'll always be receptive to you and your ideas.

Don't get the wrong idea about the data you're collecting for your little black notebook. The information you record in it is not to be used for unethical purposes. You are gathering information only to find out what the other person wants so you can help him or her get it.

The two key individuals who are vital to your career success are your own boss, and, in turn, her boss. So, find out everything you can about them: their likes and dislikes; their odd quirks and idiosyncrasies; their customs and habits; their strong points and their weak ones.

2. *How you can help your boss get what he wants.* When you know what your boss likes, then help him get it. If he's a bug about getting reports in early, then get them in early. If he wants his desk completely cleared off by quitting time, then help him get that done.

If she frowns on people coming in late, then never be late. Whatever she wants, help her get it. She's the one you want to keep happy and contented.

I want to stress that while you are creating a strong alliance with your boss and with his boss by making sure they get what they want, don't make enemies of those who can't do anything for you at the moment.

Things always change. Promotion, retirement, death, dismissal, transfer—any of these can change the status quo in a moment. So always be prepared for any eventuality. No matter what happens in the circles of executive and management power, be ready to jump in any direction and you'll always come out on top.

SOLUTIONS: HOW TO READ THE "INVISIBLE" COMPANY POWER CHART

Every company or corporation has two power charts. The official one shows the line-and-staff organization structure.

It is available for any manager or executive to read and study. This chart is described in an organizational manual, usually called the company SOP (Standing—not Standard—Operating Procedure). Formal power, command, and authority lines and positions are clearly shown.

The unofficial power chart is invisible. You can't find it on paper anywhere to study it, but it's still there. You can understand this chart only by constant and careful observation of personnel actions and activities. Since this is the real power chart, it will affect promotions and raises, retirements, resignations, and dismissals.

The power lines in the invisible chart are formed by office politics. If you want to get ahead and stay there, you must thoroughly and carefully study and understand this invisible but very real power structure. Here are some things to watch for. You may find others in your particular organization, but these points are usually common to all companies:

1. ***Who is the real information source?*** Rumors and gossip often flow rampant through all levels of the organization. However, dependable information will normally come from someone who sets policy or makes decisions, or from an individual close to that person.

Be aware that the person in authority on the official power chart may not make the final decision on a crucial matter. If he doesn't make the official decisions, it's up to you to find out who the real power source is; who's behind the scenes pulling the strings of the puppet.

2. ***Who in the organization socializes with the power elite?*** People who work together do not always play together. Most social relationships are established by membership in some organization outside the company. The connection can be political, religious, even athletic. It can result from lodge or club membership. It may also be the result of the social standing of one's spouse. Whatever the relationship is, it gives that person an edge on power

and an "in" with those who really count. Be smart; know who all these people are. Keep your guard up and watch your tongue at all times when around them.

3. ***Find out which employee has real authority in the invisible power line.*** It can come as a complete surprise to you to discover that someone outside the official power structure has the authority to either okay or kill a project. Without his initials of approval, a proposal or recommendation will die.

When I first went to work as a junior executive with a big company, I submitted a recommendation to my superior for cutting production costs in a particular department. "Take it to B. J.," he said. "Get his approval first."

"B. J.?" I said, surprised at his remark. "Why? He doesn't have any authority whatever in this area."

"You're wrong," my boss said. "B. J. doesn't have any 'official' authority in any specific area, but he's been here since the place first opened. People joke behind his back and say he's older than dirt, but the boss values his judgment highly. Without his initials of approval on your proposal, your recommendation won't get anywhere."

4. ***Who's related to whom in the company power structure?*** These people have an "in" simply because of a blood tie or a marriage relationship. If two people are equal in qualifications and ability but one of them is the boss's nephew or his wife's cousin, guess who's going to be promoted when only one opening is available.

So keep an eye on relatives of any kind. They may be powerless today, but they could have great power and authority tomorrow, even though it could be agency or borrowed power, as discussed earlier.

SOLUTIONS: HOW TO USE OFFICE POLITICS TO MAKE FRIENDS INSTEAD OF ENEMIES

Politicians aren't the only people who practice politics. Just what is politics, anyway? In the business world, good politics means getting along with people—your superiors, your associates, your subordinates, your customers or clients—and getting things done.

One of the quickest ways to make enemies in business is to practice the wrong kind of office politics by trying to seek personal gain at someone else's expense. Here's an example of how this kind of office politics can backfire:

Earl's boss, Allen, was away on summer vacation, and Earl was placed in temporary charge of the department. During Allen's absence, his boss asked for some information from his department. Earl thought this would be an excellent opportunity to impress Allen's boss with his own work and show him at the same time how undependable Allen actually was.

"Allen was hoping you wouldn't ask for this information until he got back from vacation, so he put off doing it," Earl told the big boss. "But I'll be glad to get it for you. I'll have a report to you this afternoon."

In one stroke, Earl thought he had lowered Allen's standing and raised his own prestige in the eyes of the boss. But when Allen returned from vacation, his superior called him in and told him about the incident.

"I think we'd better keep an eye on Earl," he said. "I don't believe he can be trusted. It could well be he's already reached the top of his ability. We might even have to let him go. In fact, if anything like this happens again, I'll get rid of him."

If Earl had used the right office politics, he wouldn't have created this problem for himself. All he needed to say when Allen's boss called for the information was something like this:

"Allen was gathering information for you on this just before he left on vacation. He was so swamped with last-minute work, he gave me the job to do. He said to be sure to have the report ready for you when or if you called for it. I'll make a few last-minute changes and get it to you in an hour. All the material is assembled, waiting for the final copy to be typed."

This approach would have made Earl a real comer in the eyes of Allen's boss. It would have shown that he was reliable and efficient—a person who could be depended on to get the job done in the absence of his superior.

But as will so often happen when a person tries to undercut someone else to get ahead, he ended up cutting himself instead, and there isn't a bandage big enough to cover that kind of a cut.

PROBLEM #4

BECOMING A BETTER BOSS

SOLUTIONS: AVOID THE PROBLEMS BOSSES CREATE FOR THEMSELVES

A great many times you'll discover that your employees are not causing your problems; you are creating them yourself. As the old cliché goes, "We have met the enemy, and he is us!"

To help you from falling into that trap, here is a list of the most common gripes people have against their bosses so you can avoid making these same mistakes. I'm not going to give you any specific solutions for these complaints. I think the answers are self-evident.

1. "My boss treats me like a piece of office equipment. He makes me feel stupid in front of others. He has absolutely no knowledge whatever of human relationships."

2. "Whenever I make a mistake, my boss doesn't have the courtesy to correct me in private. She yells at me in front of all my co-workers and makes me feel like a worthless nobody."

3. "She's always making promises to get people to do things for her, but then she never keeps her word."

4. "My boss isn't fair. He plays favorites and they're the ones who get the promotions, pay raises, and special privileges. With him it isn't what you know, but whether he likes you or not that counts."

5. "He never says thanks or gives a compliment to anyone. It'd be nice to hear him say just once in a while what a good job I've done for him."

6. "She's really disorganized. Tells you something one day and then denies she ever said it the next day. You never know which way you're going with her."

7. "He always passes the buck to someone else when he makes a mistake. He wants all the credit when the job is done right, but he won't accept any of the blame when things go wrong."

8. "He discriminates against older people and women."

9. "He's made a pass at every woman in the place. Thinks he's God's gift to every single woman between twenty and thirty. It's not even safe to go into the coffee room if he's around."

10. "My boss doesn't have the courage to stand for what she knows to be right. She waffles all over the place trying to compromise and please everybody."

11. "He's two-faced—tells me what a good job I'm doing and then tells others I'm the worst secretary he's ever had!"

How can you keep from making these same mistakes? Do the complete opposite of what those various bosses did.

SOLUTIONS: ALWAYS TELL THE TRUTH AND KEEP YOUR WORD

The other day I read an article called "Ten Commandments for Executives and Managers." It said that to be an effective executive or manager, you must gain the respect of your people, be a good listener, help people solve their problems, practice the Golden Rule, control your temper, know how to motivate people, know each person individually, forgive and forget. But nowhere did I find a commandment that you should always tell the truth and keep your word.

Later on I read another article entitled "Twenty-Five Ways to Recognize the Perfect Supervisor." Some of the guidelines mentioned were that a good supervisor makes people want to do things, pinpoints priorities, emphasizes the positive, follows up and follows through, helps people grow, is receptive to new ideas, and so on. Again, nowhere did I find even the barest mention of the fact that a perfect supervisor always tells the truth and keeps his word.

So my curiosity was aroused. I read more articles and scanned several excellent books on leadership, supervision, and management, yet nowhere did any one of these authors even mention telling the truth and keeping one's word.

I thought, *Am I getting old-fashioned? Am I completely out of date?* I'd always felt that telling the truth and keeping my word were absolutely fundamental in my relationships with others. In fact, I can still remember my father's lecture when I made the mistake of lying to him for the first and only time.

"The most important attribute a man can have is character, son," he said. "Without character, a man is nothing. A man of character is always able to know right from wrong and he will have the courage to adhere to the right. He is a man of honor . . . a man to be trusted . . . a man of his word. He will not lie, cheat, or steal. He is a person of good repute. No man can climb above the limitations of his own character. Remember that and never lie to anyone again."

But the authors of all those articles and books on leadership, supervision, and management evidently felt that honesty and integrity, telling the truth and keeping your word, were old-fashioned, out-of-date concepts.

If they are old fashioned, out-of-date concepts, why is there such a credibility gap between government leaders and the people? Why do we consider a politician's solemn pledges as little more than a bunch of "campaign promises" or, worse yet, outright lies? Why is there such a deep public distrust of government agencies, corporations, manufacturers, warranties, and guarantees? Why do we need people like Ralph Nader? Why does the consumer need to be protected?

My conclusion was simply this: to keep your word, to tell the truth at all times might not always be popular, but they are both still highly important.

So at the risk of sounding old-fashioned and out of date, I decided to include the following pages in this book. If you feel you don't need to read them, congratulations. But if you do decide to read and follow my advice, here are some of the benefits that you will gain for yourself:

✔ *People will believe what you say.* When you gain the reputation of telling the truth and keeping your word, people will believe what you say and they'll do what you ask them to do, knowing it's the right thing.

✔ *You'll have the reputation of being dependable.* When you are reliable, when your performance can always be depended on with absolute certainty by your boss—he will rely on you more and more to get the job done, for he knows he can trust you.

✔ *You'll be respected by everyone.* A person who tells the truth, who keeps his word, who never breaks her promises is respected by everyone. You can have a lot of other faults that people will overlook as long as they know you are telling them the truth. It's hard to criticize a person or to be angry with him when he admits he's wrong and accepts the blame without question when he's at fault. Such a person is always highly respected by others. Always tell the truth and keep your word so you can be that person.

✔ *You won't have to remember what you said.* At first glance, this might not seem to be much of a benefit, but it's truly a big one. People who don't tell the truth are constantly in a dither trying to remember what they said to others. Tell the truth and you won't have to memorize what you said.

And now for the techniques you can use to make sure you always do tell the truth and keep your word:

1. *Make your word your bond.* If you want to be a top-level executive, be as good as your word and your word must be your bond. To make sure you keep your word to others, keep these three simple points in mind:

✔ Never make a promise that you cannot keep.

✔ Never make a decision that you cannot support.

✔ Never issue an order that you can't enforce.

2. *Practice absolute honesty and truthfulness in everything at all times.* Don't allow yourself the luxury of even one tiny white lie.

3. *Be accurate and correct in everything you say.*

4. *Your signature on any document is your certification as to the truthfulness of that document.* For instance, when you write a personal check, your signature is a certificate to the effect that you have enough money in the bank to cover that check. Your signature in your work and in your business must carry exactly the same weight.

5. *Stand for what you believe to be right.* Have the courage of your convictions, regardless of the consequences. Never compromise your standards; never prostitute your principles.

6. *Duty and honor always come first.* If ever you are tempted to compromise your principles, then you must place honesty and your sense of duty and personal honor above all else.

SOLUTIONS: WORK AT BEING RESPECTED, NOT LIKED

We all want to be liked and have people think well of us. Managers and executives are no exception to this rule. But if you try to make a career out of just being liked, you're making a big mistake. It's far more important that you gain the respect of all your subordinates. Then chances are they'll like you, too.

Here is an example of why it's a mistake to try to be liked rather than respected. Gary B. was promoted to the position of supervisor from the labor force in a large carpet and rug manufacturing company. He was retained in the same department so the company could use his technical skills and experience to the maximum.

Gary wanted to succeed in his new job, but he was also anxious to keep his friendships intact with his former co-workers. He didn't want them to think he was putting on airs and trying to lord it over them.

Gary continued to go to a local bar for a few beers with his men when they got off work. He rolled the dice with them for drinks just as before. Sometimes a few beers became too many, and when a man drank too much, Gary gave him the morning off, knowing he'd be useless at work with a hangover anyway.

So the word spread that nothing had changed. "No sweat," the men told each other. "Gary is the same old Gary. Promotion to supervisor hasn't changed him one bit." And Gary did find it hard to reprimand a man or discipline him at work when he'd been partying with him the night before.

He overlooked their mistakes more and more. He let them get by with prolonging their coffee breaks and lunch periods. Nor did he say anything when people were late to work. He accepted all sorts of excuses for absenteeism. He even approved work that he would have been ashamed of doing a few short weeks before.

In less than two months after Gary had taken over the department, it was in complete shambles. Production had fallen off, quality had slipped badly, accidents had increased, several hundred yards of expensive fabric had been ruined, housekeeping had become sloppy and slipshod, the men were careless about everything.

So the plant manager called for Gary. "I've been waiting for you to get on your feet and get things under control," he said. "I realized you were new on the job and I wanted to give you every opportunity to get things organized and straightened out, but I can't wait any longer. You have thirty days to get your department back in shape. If you don't, you're through."

Naturally, Gary was scared. He'd tried to be a good fellow and he'd failed to get the job done. So he figured he'd have to be an SOB to succeed. He tried to regain control by tightening the screws and getting tough with his men, but it was too late.

They rebelled completely. There was flagrant disobedience of orders; machinery broke down for lack of oil and water; maintenance and repair people found wrenches and screwdrivers jammed into wheels and gear boxes.

So management gave up on Gary. They figured the only way to get the department back under control was to start over with a brand-new supervisor—a complete stranger—and that's what they did.

Gary made the mistake of trying to assume the responsibilities of a new position as the boss of his former co-workers and trying to retain the same old friendly relationships with them at the same time. The result was total failure. It didn't work for Gary and it won't work for you. It never does.

Admittedly, company management made a mistake, too. They would have been far better off not to keep Gary in the same department when they promoted him, even though they wanted to utilize his special technical skills and abilities in that department, but that isn't the real reason for Gary's failure.

Gary was still primarily at fault, for *he placed more emphasis on being liked than on being respected.* Therefore, he could only *demand* respect. Had he placed more emphasis on being respected than on being liked, he'd have been able to *command* respect instead of demanding it.

Here are some techniques you can use to avoid a fate like Gary's:

1. *Don't* accept favors from your subordinates. This is a standing rule—even though sometimes violated—in the armed services, government, and in most companies. The point is, the moment you accept a favor from a subordinate, you're obligating yourself to do one for him in return. At any level, this can lead to inefficiency, blackmail, bribery, and corruption.

2. *Don't* do special favors, trying to be liked. This doesn't mean you shouldn't help your people do their jobs whenever and however you can. But it does mean you shouldn't overlook a person's faults on the job, his bad work, tardiness, absenteeism, and the like as a special favor to him.

3. *Don't* try to make popular decisions. Popularity is short lived. Your job is to be a manager—not to win some popularity contest.

4. *Don't* be soft about enforcing discipline. If a person knows the punishment for a certain act but he does it anyway, don't let him off the hook just because you feel sorry for him. If you don't stick to your principles, he'll do it again and again. So punish with compassion and justice, but punish, period, when it's warranted.

5. *Don't* party or socialize with your subordinates. Sure, it's nice to be well liked by the people who work for you, but social relationships with your employees will interfere with your company responsibilities. *When the boss gets involved socially with his subordinates, he's no longer the boss.*

6. *Don't* place yourself in a compromising position with your employees. If you follow the first five *Don'ts,* chances are you won't find yourself in this pickle. This problem can come up when a manager decides to take money under the table, accepts a gift from a subordinate or a supplier, gets romantically involved with an employee, or any number of things along this line. You leave yourself wide open for at least petty blackmail, perhaps even worse.

SOLUTIONS: SET THE EXAMPLE FOR OTHERS TO FOLLOW

Leaders are examples to be followed, not models to be admired. Setting the example to be followed is not an easy task. It means developing such personal traits as courage, integrity, tact, unselfishness, dependability, and a host of others. It means sticking to what you know to be morally right even when it would be easier not to.

As Albert Schweitzer, the famed medical missionary who established a hospital in Africa, once said, "Example is not the main thing in life, it is the only thing." So set the proper example and you won't have to preach a sermon to your subordinates. They'll need only follow in your footsteps to do the right thing.

Your people will look to you as the example to be followed. If you set a poor example, they'll use you as an excuse for their mistakes and shortcomings.

But if you set the proper example by your own conduct, they'll respect you and want to live up to your standards. Here are some techniques you can use:

Set a high standard for subordinates to follow.

"I myself must set the standard in all things for my employees to follow," says Maxine Randall, the manager of one of the biggest department stores in Atlanta, Georgia. "And confidence in the successful completion of a difficult job or the achievement of a specific sales goal is one of the most important ways that I, as a manager, can set that example.

"By my every act and word I must show my own confidence in the successful outcome of a tough project. If I show the least bit of doubt, I'll cause my people to have doubts of their own. Success, then, is not likely to follow. So setting the standard of confidence is an important part of my job as a manager."

This same idea applies to many other relationships with your people, too. For instance, you want them to be courteous, respectful, loyal, and cooperative. So you must set the example by showing them courtesy, respect, loyalty, and cooperation with them first. You must lead the way.

If you are irregular in your own work habits, late for your appointments, careless about safety rules, and apparently bored with your work, the people under you will follow your example and act the same way.

On the other hand, if you're punctual in coming to work and on time for your appointments, if you obey the safety rules yourself, if you're enthusiastic about your work, if you set a high standard by your own stellar performance of duty, they'll want to follow your good example.

Remember that any organization is an accurate mirror of the viewpoints, strengths, confidences, fears, and shortcomings of its leader. Therefore, you must set the standard and the example in all things. It can be no other way.

Set the example by working hard.

"One of the best ways to set the example is to work hard yourself," says Robert Doyle, the safety director for the Budd Company of Pittsburgh. "Few things will command more attention than plain, old-fashioned hard work. Stop thinking about what you can get out of your job and concentrate on what you can put into it for a change.

"Put out some extra effort. Skip your coffee break or have your coffee at your desk once in a while. Shorten your lunch hour. Come to work early part of the time. Stay until your desk is clear at night. Be willing to go beyond the call of duty—to go the extra mile. Try that for just one month. Your job efficiency will skyrocket. And let me tell you this, too. The person who works hard—every day of the week and every hour of the day when he or she is on the job—is still rare enough to stand out in any group."

Use your initiative.

Initiative is the power of taking the first step, of seeing what has to be done and commencing a course of action, even in the absence of orders. As Hannibal, the Carthaginian general who was one of the greatest military geniuses of all time, said, "I will find a way or I will make one." Your people will unite behind you quickly when you meet unexpected situations with prompt and decisive action.

You can encourage initiative among your people by assigning them work commensurate with their abilities and then allowing them to work out the details and finish the job.

Closely associated with initiative is resourcefulness, the ability to deal with a situation or solve a problem in the absence of normal means or methods. Inactivity or passive acceptance of an unsatisfactory situation because you lack conventional methods of handling it is never justified.

Here are eight ways you can use your initiative to get the job done and set the example for your people to follow at the same time:

1. Stay mentally and physically alert.

2. Train yourself to recognize tasks that need to be done and then do them without being told to do so.

3. Think up new approaches to problems.

4. Learn to anticipate by thinking ahead.

5. Make the most of promising new ideas or plans.

6. Look for and readily accept responsibility.

7. Encourage your employees to try new methods and new ideas.

8. Utilize all your available resources in the most effective and efficient manner possible.

"Credibility gaps have become extremely common today, not only in government, but also in business and industry between the leaders and their people," says Merle Riley, the Chief Purchasing Officer for a large Kansas City corporation.

"A person who tells it like it is, no matter what the consequences to himself, or who isn't trying to milk some special privileges and advantages out of his position—especially at the expense of his subordinates—will be highly regarded by his employees."

You'll pull your employees up to your level.

Employees imitate the boss and pick up her habits. They are inclined to do as their superior does and follow her example, good or bad.

When you don't use your management position for personal gain, your subordinates will emulate you. Honesty will increase; petty thievery will decrease. Your own integrity on the job will set a positive example for them to follow. You will motivate and inspire people to pull themselves up to your high standards. Here are some techniques you can use to gain these benefits:

1. ***Practice the old-fashioned virtue of honesty.*** The moment you are guilty of any dishonest act, no matter how slight, whenever you take anything at all for your own personal use without paying for it, no matter how small, you weaken your moral authority over your subordinates. You'll lose their respect and it will be extremely difficult to regain it.

"Sometimes you'll take the item without even thinking about it and then pay the penalty later," says Henry Sanders, the director of safety in a West Coast navy shipyard.

"For example, the second morning after I took over this job, the chief storekeeper came by and wanted to know my shoe size. When I came back from lunch, I found a brand-new pair of expensive safety shoes on my desk.

"Well, I was busy learning a new job so I stuck them down in a desk drawer and forgot all about them. A week later my secretary stuck her head in my door and said, 'The chief storekeeper, Mr. Hobbs, would like to see you.'

"Mr. Hobbs came in, sat down without being asked to do so, leisurely lighted up a cigarette, smiled expansively at me, and said,

You might be surprised to discover that I have not discussed suc personal qualities as bearing, dress, language, morals, and the sort o things we normally call "Sunday School virtues" to set the example fo others to follow. Don't misunderstand me. I have nothing against thes fine qualities. Nor do I feel they're not important—I certainly do.

However, first of all, I'm not qualified to tell you what to do o what not to do in your own personal behavior. Second, I'm the onl person in the world whose morals I have to concern myself with.

SOLUTIONS: NEVER USE YOUR POSITION FOR PERSONAl GAIN

Frank McGee, the popular NBC newscaster for many years and th host on the *Today* show after Hugh Downs left, once said, "Whe all other motives fail, you can always depend on greed."

Nearly every day in your newspaper, you can read about pec ple in exceptionally high places who let their greed get the best o them and used their positions for personal gain: big-city mayors labor union leaders, businesspeople, senators, members o Congress, military officers—even ministers.

By not using your management position for personal gain you'll achieve some powerful benefits:

You can live with yourself.

"Not that I'm any paragon of virtue; I'm not," says Roger Johnson, the national sales director for a large chemical company. "But I can honestly say I've never used my executive position for personal gain. I've never had to worry about an auditor going over my records or checking my cash funds, or a security guard opening my briefcase or the trunk of my car, anything like that. And I can sleep without the aid of sleeping pills. I can live with myself."

Your subordinates will trust you.

When your subordinates know you're not using your management position for personal gain, they'll trust you and have confidence in you. You'll gain their loyalty and their wholehearted support.

'How are your new shoes? Do they fit you all right? Is there anything else you need?'

"As I looked at him, his face seemed to assume the features of a larcenous old army supply sergeant who'd gotten to me when I was a young and inexperienced second lieutenant.

"When I took command of my first company at Fort Leonard Wood, he loaded down my desk with fatigue uniforms, combat boots, field jackets, blankets, sheets—all those expensive but necessary things young second lieutenants can't afford.

"Like a fool, I took everything he had to offer. And for the next six months, he had me in his pocket. He had me right where he wanted me. I made the mistake of thinking all officers were entitled to such privileges when, of course, they weren't.

"Remembering that experience and not wanting to repeat it, I said to Mr. Hobbs, 'How much do those safety shoes cost?'

"'To you, nothing,' he said. 'Consider them a gift.'

"'But who paid for them?' I asked.

'The company,' he said. 'But that's all right. I'm entitled to a small operating loss to cover things like that.'

"'Do other employees here in the shipyard pay for them?'

"'Oh yes,' he said. 'They cost them $54 a pair, but after all, you're the safety director, so there's no cost to you.'

"'Do I have to wear them?' I asked.

"'Of course,' he said. 'They're required in the work area.'

"'Then prepare the proper bill for them,' I said, 'or take them back and I'll buy a pair somewhere else. I will not accept them from you as a gift.'"

Refuse such gifts from your subordinates just as Henry Sanders did. There are too many strings attached, and you don't want to be the puppet dangling from the end of them.

2. **You, too, must follow the rules.** Sometimes managers forget that the rules are for them to follow, too. Employees will certainly notice if a foreman or a supervisor is smoking a cigarette in a nonsmoking area. And speaking of smoking reminds me of an incident a friend of mine told me the other day:

"I'd found some marijuana in my son's jacket pocket," J. L. said, "and I was giving him a lecture about why he shouldn't be using it, like how we don't know enough about its effects on the mind and the body, and how it could lead to the use of hard drugs. I ended up saying whether it was harmful or not was beside the point, for after all, the use of marijuana was against the law.

"But Jeff really stopped me cold when he said, 'So was cheating on your income tax last year when you claimed Mary as a dependent even though she got married the year before. But that was different, Dad, wasn't it?'"

So you see, you must follow the rules, too. Telling your people to do what you want them to do isn't enough. They won't listen to you, especially if your actions are different from your words. They'll do as you do or as they want to do.

3. ***Don't abuse your privileges.*** None of your subordinates will object to the extra privileges that go with your office as long as you use your position to guard and protect their interests, too. But they will object strenuously when you assume privileges that are not rightfully and legitimately yours.

For instance, the army officer who uses government transportation to get from his quarters to his work or eats in a company mess hall without paying for it or uses an enlisted man as a personal servant is despised by all his men. So is the traveling sales rep who pads her expense account, or the plant manager who uses company materials and labor for his own private benefit.

Your subordinates expect you to play your part to the letter. They'll never take exception to your title, your position, your prerogatives, or your privileges as long as you don't abuse them. Your management position was created to allow you to fulfill your responsibility to your superiors by serving your subordinates. Think of it that way and you can't possibly go wrong.

Making Yourself Into a Leader

SOLUTIONS: HOW TO DEVELOP THE TRAITS OF LEADERSHIP

To supervise and control people successfully, *you must first be a leader.* Some people think that leaders are born, not made. That is not true at all. However, there are five character traits that must be deeply ingrained, almost inborn, in a person, if that person is to lead others successfully.

Here, then, are the traits you must develop to become a leader of others. These are the specific characteristics that top executives look for when they select those to promote to higher responsibilities in leadership and management positions:

1. *Character is your first essential trait.* If you have character, you will instinctively know the difference between right and wrong. Not only will you know the right thing to do, you will also have the courage to do it. You will be a person of honor. You are to be trusted. You will not lie, cheat, or steal, no matter what advantage you would gain by doing so.

2. *You must possess the power of decision.* You must be able to make a decision. It is not enough that you use logic and rea-

son to make an evaluation of the situation. Many people can do that. But only a rare few can make a decision at the right time and then announce it without hesitation. Today's leadership problems will never be solved with yesterday's solutions.

3. **You need wisdom to plan and order.** Once you make your decision, you must develop a workable plan to carry it out. Definite and specific tasks must be given to your people. Your plan must answer certain specific questions: What is to be done? Who will do it? Where, when, and how will it be done? The wisdom to plan and order is one of the essential traits you will need to be a leader of others.

4. **You must have the courage to act.** Even though you have the ability to make sound decisions and excellent plans and orders based on those decisions, you will still be far from gaining your goals unless you have the courage to act. The brilliant thinker with the faint heart invites only disaster through inaction or hesitancy. You must have the courage to do what has to be done, despite the costs, hardships, hazards, and sacrifices.

Though you might have vision to see what needs to be done and the wisdom of Solomon to help you in making those decisions, you'll not get the results you want unless you have the courage to act when action is required to succeed.

5. **You must have the ability to manage.** To be a leader of others, you must develop the ability to manage. The ability to manage is the systematic approach to the attainment of specific goals. It requires administrative skill and know-how. Management is a tool of good leadership.

It's easy to take the perfect combination of an abundant and well-trained workforce, all the desired supplies and equipment, unlimited funds, and indefinite time to complete a project. That's no challenge at all; anyone can do that.

The real challenge to your management ability comes when you have to make the best use of whatever you have on hand to do what has to be done. You'll be measured by what you can accomplish under adverse circumstances.

Now that you know the five character traits you need to fully develop to become a leader of others, I'll show you how to use these leadership tools to control large groups of people.

SOLUTIONS: HOW TO CONTROL LARGE GROUPS OF PEOPLE

There are two powerful techniques you can use to control large numbers of people. One is to give everyone a specific job to do; get them all involved. The other is to use the proper span of control.

Let me discuss first the principle of *giving everyone a specific job to do*. When you give people something worthwhile and meaningful to do, something that will keep them physically as well as mentally occupied, they'll be happy and contented with their work. This technique works for ministers as well as for anyone else, if they understand the principle of application as well as Reverend Price Jennings does.

"Most ministers complain they can't keep young people between eighteen and thirty interested in the church," Reverend Jennings says. "Do you know why they can't? They don't give them a job to do; that's why. Religion consists of two W's: *Worship* and *Work*. And they must be properly balanced. You can't keep young people coming with too much preaching from you and too little work from them.

"Young people are interested in developing a better world for themselves. They know they can't do that with a couple of hymns, a prayer, and sermon on Sunday morning. They know that worship alone just isn't enough. It takes a lot of work, too.

"Our church is crammed and overflowing with young men and women because we offer them participation—not substitution. The goal of our youth activity program is to make the communities we live in better. So we worship in the church; we work in our neighborhoods.

"A Christmas and Thanksgiving basket for the poor family is not the answer. It takes much more than that. For instance, I watched Charles Kuralt, the former traveling CBS newsman, report on how people in Las Vegas, Nevada, got together and built a much needed city park in a poor neighborhood in just about twenty-four hours.

"How'd they do that? Well, everybody, young and old, rich and poor, black and white, yellow, red, and brown, Catholic and Protestant, pitched in and helped. Everybody had a job to do and they did it. That's how. That's the kind of thing I mean."

Next I want to discuss with you how to use the correct *span of control* to lead large groups of people. When you use the proper span of control, you'll be able to control many people through your subordinate leaders. Genghis Khan controlled his vast far-flung empire through certain key people: his loyal tribal chieftains. The President of General Motors has an organization with thousands of employees whom he controls with the help of key executives and able administrators.

What, then, is the span of control? It is the number of immediate subordinates that one person can control, supervise, and direct effectively. One of the factors that influences the span of control is the ability of a person to divide his attention between two or more tasks. Each of us has an upper limit beyond which we cannot give our attention to any more work, no matter how pressing or important. Even below this upper limit, assignment of any new job tends to detract from the efficient accomplishment of those tasks already at hand. Not only that, our ability to divide attention decreases as mental or physical exhaustion increases. So the maximum span of control diminishes rapidly with increased mental or physical fatigue.

"Don't violate the span of control if you want to lead large numbers of people successfully," says William Hartline, the president of Republic Lumber Company, a chain of building supply centers. "As long as you don't violate the span of control, the total number of people you employ or supervise has little or no actual bearing on your ability to lead people. The span of control is the number of *immediate subordinates* that one person can control, supervise, or direct effectively.

"Most management consultants feel that the economically minimum span of control is three. Give a person less than three immediate subordinates to supervise and there will be too little to do; you'll not be getting your money's worth.

"They also set the maximum span of control for the average supervisor at eight immediate subordinates. If that number is exceeded, your organization will become unwieldy and hard to manage. Efficiency will go downhill rapidly.

"The number of immediate subordinates you supervise is the key to the correct span of control," Mr. Hartline goes on to say. "That is the key to knowing how to control and supervise large numbers of employees as I do. For instance, you could easily control eight hundred employees through your own eight immediate subordinate leaders.

"You see, those eight immediate subordinates of yours will in turn have eight immediate subordinates of their own to help them establish their controls over people. When you've superimposed that span of control over your whole organization, from the top clear down to the very bottom, graphically it would look like a pyramid or a triangle with you standing all alone at the very top. Company, corporation, business of any kind, army division, air wing, whatever, it's all the same."

Mr. Hartline has 125 separate building supply centers and more than 1,500 employees. Yet his organization span of control is set up so that no executive, foreman, or supervisor has more than eight subordinates to lead and control.

Although one foreman might have more than a hundred people in his department, his span of control is organized so that he himself has only eight supervisors reporting to him. And each of those supervisors will have no more than eight employees reporting to him, and so on down the line.

If you are having trouble controlling the people you supervise and are responsible for, check your span of control. If you have more than eight immediate subordinates to supervise, that's no doubt where your problem lies, for you can't pay attention to the work of any more than eight people.

SOLUTIONS: HOW TO GET THE KEY WORKERS ON YOUR SIDE

In addition to using the span of control, you need to get non-supervisory personnel on your side before you can succeed in management. These key people are the informal leaders among the "blue collar" workers.

In every group of rank-and-file employees, you'll find certain persons to whom the others turn for advice, help, and leadership. For instance, I've seen this actually happen: A supervisor in management issues an order, turns his back, and walks away. Immediately, the workers in that group gather around one key individual. He speaks; they listen. Then they go back to work and carry out the supervisor's order. *But not until they get the unofficial go-ahead from the informal leader of their group.*

The speed of production and quality of workmanship will depend not only upon the order from the supervisor in management but also on the order from the informal leader in labor.

So if you want to get the best out of all your people, if you want to get all your line production workers to cooperate with you, find out who those informal leaders in labor are. Do that, and you'll be able to save much time and energy by concentrating your efforts through your management people on those individuals in labor who can help you achieve your goals.

Once you know who the key people in labor are, you can use them as your unofficial communication system. You can have your managers, your foremen, and line supervisors feel out their groups by taking those key people aside and getting their opinions and ideas first. This doesn't make them the boss or take away any authority from your managers. It simply gets those key people in labor on your side from the beginning. The basic rule is this: *Find out who the informal leaders in labor are and get them on your side first; the rest will automatically follow.*

Above all, don't let your managers lock horns with these key individuals. There's nothing wrong with their having influence in their groups as long as they don't misuse their power and try to usurp yours. You'll get much farther if you work with these people and use the power they have with their groups to your own advantage.

Here are some clues as to how you can recognize and identify these key people in the ranks of labor:

1. *A key person will be the unofficial leader of the group.* This individual is part of the unofficial power chart found in *every* organization. He wields an influence that has no relationship at all to his actual position. Though he's not part of the official power line of authority, a word from him can make or break a project.

2. *A key person will be an independent individual.* You can usually spot a key person in the group by her need for independent action. A great many times, this key individual will be a woman who has refused a position of management or supervision—even though she apparently has all the necessary leadership qualifications—simply because she doesn't want to be pinned down by official responsibility. She wants to be free to operate without being hampered by administrative rules and regulations or organizational red tape.

3. *The key person is a problem solver.* A key individual will often have a solution for your problem. Many times the hardest part of solving any problem is simply getting started on it. Often what you need are suggestions to help you solve your problem, no matter where those ideas come from or who supplies them. A key person will usually have several suggestions to make. Her ideas may not always be the exact solutions that you need, but they will help you get things moving again in a bogged-down situation. And as the old saying goes, "A poor plan carried out enthusiastically is better than the best plan that is not carried out at all."

4. *The key person is a creative thinker.* A key individual will be a creative thinker—a true nonconformist. A really creative person will be a wellspring of ideas. He will resist any efforts to restrict and channel his thinking. If his creative urge is strong enough, it will show up in his efforts to get transferred to challenging jobs or, at the least, to acquire additional knowledge of other departments and other people's work. This may well be your first clue to the presence of a key person who can help you solve your problems and gain your goals.

So, no matter how many persons you work with or how many are in the group you need to influence and control, it's essential that you locate these key people in labor before you try to do anything else. They can get the needed action for you when and where you need it most.

SOLUTIONS: HOW TO HANDLE THE REAL PROBLEM PERSON

First of all, it's important that you know how to determine whether a person who works for you actually is or is not a problem to you. A lot of people will disagree on this basic point. Some will say that a problem person is anyone who is abnormal or maladjusted. Others will say the problem person is a nonconformist, an offbeat individual who speaks, thinks, or acts differently from the way the majority of people do. Many people tend to classify any individual with long hair or a beard as a problem person.

A person could fit into any of these categories and still not be a problem to you or anyone else. As Thoreau once said, "If a man does not keep pace with his companions, perhaps it is because he hears a different drummer. Let him step to the music which he hears, however measured or far away."

No matter what others say about someone who works for you, you need answer only one question to determine whether that person is or is not a problem to you. *Is this person causing you damage or harm in some way?* If he is, then he's a problem to you and you should do something to correct this situation. But if he's not causing you tangible harm or damage, *no matter what his appearance, dress, or personal behavior,* then you don't have a problem person on your hands after all, so you need do absolutely nothing about him.

Whatever you think, don't let personal dislikes or prejudices about the color of a person's skin, short skirts, or beards and mustaches mislead you. If you do that, you're trying to judge people by your own personal standards of right and wrong.

When you understand this simple concept of what a problem person really is, you're actually much better informed in this business of handling problem people than are a lot of personnel managers or industrial relations people who make this a full-time job.

The problem person, however, can create trouble for you at work. He or she can cause you harm or damage by hurting your production, your sales, or your profits. All you need do is ask yourself three simple questions. If you cannot answer yes to at least one of them, then this person is not a problem to you.

1. *Is his or her job performance below your established standards?* Is the person's work below the accepted norm in either quality or quantity? Does the person produce fewer units than others in an average work day? Does the person have more work rejected by quality control than anyone else? Does the person always have fewer sales than other salespeople do at the end of the week? *Does this individual fail in some specific way to measure up to the reasonable performance standards you've set and that all others are able to meet?* If so, then this person is costing you money and you definitely have a problem person on your hands.

2. ***Does she interfere with the performance of others?*** Is this person a constant source of irritation, annoyance, or interference? Do you usually find her in the middle of employee disturbances? Does she keep other people from doing their best work? Does the quality or the quantity of her work slow down or prevent other sections or groups from functioning properly? Does she cause some of her co-workers to lose incentive pay by her careless actions? If so, then she is a definite problem to you.

3. ***Does he cause harm to the group as a whole?*** The reputation or good name of any group can be damaged even if only one of its members is a chronic source of trouble. He can keep the rest of the group constantly on edge by what he says or does. For example, if one member of a professional athletic team gets out of line, he gives the entire team a morale problem. One troublesome sales representative can give the entire company a bad name. If any of your people have constantly caused you to get complaints, have orders cancelled, or lose good customers by carelessness, indifference, or sloppy work, you have a problem person to take care of.

How to uncover the cause of his or her problem.

You'll need to find the real reason behind what a person says or does so you can help solve the problem. *When their problem is solved, yours will go away, too.* In other words, the best way for you to solve your problem is to help them solve theirs.

You can do this by skillfully asking questions and carefully listening to the answers. Listen between the lines, too, for many times what a person does *not* say will tell you more than what he or she does say. This is not done in a formal interview from behind a desk. Your information should be subtly gathered over a period of time by informal chats, routine visits to work sites, a cup of coffee together—that sort of thing.

I have found from personal experience that the failure of an employer or a manager to fulfill his employees' or her subordinates' basic needs on the job causes more problems than anything else. For example, if you are in charge of people, do your level best to help them achieve their needs and desires on the job. Here are nine specific ways you can do that:

1. Give them full credit and recognition for their work.
2. Make sure their work is interesting and worthwhile.
3. Offer them a fair wage with salary increases.
4. Give them your full attention; show that you appreciate them.
5. Promote by merit, not by seniority alone.
6. Offer them counsel on personal problems *if they ask you to do so.*
7. Make sure they have decent physical working conditions.
8. Within reasonable limits, offer them total job security.
9. Do anything and everything you can to make them feel important, both to you and to themselves.

When you do these things, you'll have few, if any, problem persons to deal with. Fulfilling a person's basic needs and desires gives you the *secret leverage of control* you need to get rid of 99 percent of your problem cases.

One last point worth considering under the cause of problems is this: Most people resent rules and regulations that restrict their freedom and liberties. To remove that yoke of authority that problem people, as well as others, resent so much, follow this simple principle: *Rule by work; don't work by rules.* This formula will work like magic for you.

You'll have a feeling of tremendous self-accomplishment when you learn how to master difficult or problem people. It's like taking a postgraduate course in applied psychology or human relations. You'll learn new and exciting techniques to master and control the problem person.

SOLUTIONS: HOW TO MAKE SOUND AND TIMELY DECISIONS

Your ability to make sound and timely decisions will depend to a large part on how much authority your superiors have granted you. The question is this: Will you actually use the authority you've been given to make decisions or will you be paralyzed into inactivity by the fear of making a mistake?

Before you answer that question, listen to what Calvin Knight, a top-level executive with a large computer corporation, says about executive and management decision making:

"Other than financial gain, one of the primary reasons an executive or manager hungers for promotion is that the higher the position, the more power he or she will have to make bigger and more important decisions without undue outside interference. The higher position will give the person the power that is needed to get things done.

"But then, amazingly, when he does get the power he wants, his attitude changes completely and he often hesitates to use it. This reluctance shows up in his hesitation to make decisions. He hems and haws, fiddles and procrastinates, appoints a committee to study the problem, waits for further developments in the situation—in fact, he'll go out of his way to avoid making a decision of any kind that could be traced back to him.

"The executive suites of too many companies are overloaded with so-called managers who are afraid to make decisions about anything more important than the time of the morning and afternoon coffee breaks or when to let the secretary go to lunch!"

If you want to avoid joining that fainthearted crowd, develop your ability to make sound and timely decisions. Become adept at isolating the heart of the problem.

First of all, you will need good judgment so that after considering all the factors bearing on the problem and all the ways of solving it, you will be able to determine the best workable solution. And you must be farsighted enough to anticipate and plan for all the actions and reactions that will come from your decision.

"What will happen if...?" must always be the question in the back of your mind as you look over all the possible solutions to your problem so you can make a wise decision.

You also must possess the strength of character it takes to make decisions at the proper time and to announce them at the right time and place so you can get the results. Here are six easy steps you can follow to solve your executive and management problems.

1. ***Whose responsibility is it to make this decision?*** Is this your decision to make or does it actually belong to someone else? Here you must know the boundaries and limits of your job. You must

know which decisions you and you alone *must* make and which decisions your subordinates *can* make.

Don't interfere with your people's work. Let them carry out the details of their own jobs. If you do decide that no one else but you can make this decision, then prepare yourself so you can make the correct one. But if it belongs to someone else, then get rid of it. Unload it as you would a hot potato. Give the problem to the right person to solve. That in itself is a wise decision.

2. **Assemble all the facts**. If you've decided that this is your problem to solve, the first step is to gather all the facts bearing on the problem. Here are three basic techniques you can use to do that:

- ✔ *Ask questions of people*. If you ask the right persons, there's no better way of finding out the facts you need. Ask yourself questions, too. You might be surprised to find that you know some of the answers yourself.

- ✔ *Use your eyes and ears*. Don't depend entirely on the answers of other people. There's no substitute for first-hand information. What you personally see and hear is usually more reliable than second- or third-hand information.

- ✔ *Read*. Reading will greatly expand your knowledge about how to solve problems. Learn how others have dealt with similar situations. Trade journals are especially useful, for they let you concentrate your attention on your own specific field of interest and devote a great deal of space telling how others did it.

3. **Test your facts**. After you've assembled all the facts bearing on your problem, your next step is to test them by two criteria.

a. *Your first test should be for accuracy*. Are you able to verify secondhand or word-of-mouth information by personal observation, by getting the opinion of an expert, or by experimentation? Do any of the facts you've gathered contradict each other?

b. *Your second test is for relevance*. The quickest way to test a fact for relevance is to ask yourself what it contributes to the solution of your problem. If your answer is that it contributes absolutely nothing, discard it.

4. *Get rid of irrational thoughts.* Dr. Carl Arnold, a New Orleans consulting psychologist, says three mental obstacles tend to get in the way of solving problems: "These three obstacles are prejudice, preconceived ideas, and emotion.

"Prejudice makes people look at things improperly. For instance, my father always thought a man who wore a mustache couldn't be trusted, so whenever he met someone with a mustache, he immediately categorized that person as dishonest.

"Prejudice can keep you from accepting suggestions for solving problems from an employee whom you don't like. A personnel manager I know has a thing about beards. Won't hire anyone for a management job who wears a beard. I wonder how many good people he's missed hiring because of that prejudice?

"Then there's the obstacle of preconceived ideas. Preconceived ideas and prejudice are not the same, although preconceived ideas can often lead to prejudice. A preconceived idea or notion keeps a person from accepting the real truth. For instance, cigarette smokers still insist that smoking doesn't cause lung cancer even though there's plenty of evidence to the contrary. To get over this obstacle, ask yourself these questions:

✔ "Am I just assuming something to be true?"

✔ "Do the facts verify my assumption?"

✔ "Is wishful thinking getting in the way?"

✔ "Am I confusing chance with cause and effect?"

✔ "Will my assumption pass the test of logic?"

"The last obstacle is emotion," Dr. Arnold concludes. "Any strong feeling—hate, love, fear, suspicion, jealousy—interferes with the evaluation of the facts. A person who's filled with hatred for others sees every day as dark, gloomy, and miserable. A young girl in love sees the sun shining through the clouds even on the rainiest day. The rule here is never study the facts of a problem or try to solve it under emotional stress or strain."

5. *Reach a tentative solution.* This is the fifth step in solving your problem. After you've gathered your facts, weighed them, and viewed them without prejudice or passion, you should now be able to reach a tentative solution.

The best solution will normally be the one with the most advantages and the least disadvantages. You might come up with thirty-nine different ways to skin a cat, but you want the best one.

6. **Put your solution into effect by taking the necessary action.** This is the last step in your problem-solving technique, but it is often the toughest one to take because of the fear of making a mistake. But to hesitate now is foolish, to say the least. The hard work is over. Don't waver with indecision. Move right out with confidence and put your corrective action to work at once. After you've decided which solution you're going to use, put it into effect immediately by issuing the necessary order. Take the appropriate action; put your solution to work for you.

If you follow these guidelines and techniques, you'll be able to make sound and timely decisions. You won't have to call a mass meeting every time you make a decision. You'll learn to acquire all the information possible and then have the courage to say to yourself, "Now it's all up to me to decide what to do!"

When you do this, you'll get the self-starter's habit of action and leadership. You'll get things done.

DEVELOPING WORKPLACE GUIDELINES

SOLUTIONS: HOW TO GET RESULTS BY EMPHASIZING SKILLS, NOT RULES

As I mentioned, one of the best techniques you can use to get results from people is not to work by rules, but to rule by work. I want to amplify and expand that idea now.

Once upon a time there was an obedient soldier named Smith. One day when Smith's army division was in Louisiana on maneuvers, his sergeant stationed him at a lonely intersection and told him to direct traffic. Smith was instructed not to leave his post until he was properly relieved.

Three days later, when a temporary cessation of the mock hostilities had been declared, Smith's sergeant realized one man in his squad was missing—namely, Smith.

Jumping into a jeep, he hurried to the intersection where he'd left Smith. Sure enough, Smith was still there, but he was directing *civilian* traffic—not military. Hungry? Famished. Thirsty? Of course. But he'd remained faithfully at his post, never once questioning his orders.

Division officers asked Smith if he hadn't felt something could be wrong, especially when the military traffic he'd been told to direct abruptly stopped and was replaced by civilian cars.

"Yes, sir," he said. "I thought something might be wrong, but I figured it was none of my business. My sergeant told me not to leave my post until I was properly relieved. And, sir—I just hadn't been properly relieved!"

Smith's officers gave up questioning him when they heard that. It was no use. *Smith believed he was right just as long as he followed the rules.*

Diligence is not always a virtue. Were his actions commendable? Yes, in a sense, if a person is to be praised for blindly following the rules without question. But diligence and dullness don't go together. After missing two meals in a row, I would've been finding out exactly where my relief was and why he hadn't shown up to replace me.

But then I was never one to go too much by the rules just for the sake of following the rules when I was in the army, especially if they didn't make any sense. However, I've also found over my years in business and industry that the concept of rules for the sake of rules isn't confined to the military alone. Let me give you a quick example of that:

One morning I stood with a young foreman watching the change of shifts in his department. It was a few minutes before seven—the plant time for punching out on the time clock. The day shift had already reported; they'd been briefed about their current production schedule by the outgoing crew. Ready and waiting at their machines, they needed only their supervisor's nod to start work.

The outgoing shift was tired. They'd been on duty since eleven the night before. Now that they were through, they were squatting on their haunches or sitting on stacks of rubber skids waiting for the seven o'clock whistle to blow.

The young foreman called his night shift supervisor over. "Get your men on their feet," he said. "You know I don't allow anyone to sit down while he's working in my department!"

"But, Hank, my men are all through work," the supervisor said. "They're just waiting for the whistle to blow so they can go home."

"Don't talk back to me! That's an order!" the foreman yelled. "They're still on the clock, so get 'em on their feet. *Those are my rules!*"

To keep you from issuing a nonsensical order like that, here are *eight principles for rulemaking.*

1. Every rule should be aimed at accomplishing your primary mission.

2. A good rule should consider the welfare of your employees.

3. A good rule should raise their morale—not lower it.

4. The most effective rules are those your employees make to discipline their own conduct.

5. Good rules make for good discipline.

6. A good rule should improve a person's individual job proficiency.

7. Every rule should be aimed at improving your organizational efficiency.

8. Company esprit is an important indicator of the value of your rules.

In the final analysis of the value of your rules, judge your employee's actions and procedures by the end results—both in terms of increasing the competitive position of your company and the welfare of your people.

Go easy on the pat rules unless they have to do with safety. Doing it by the book isn't always the best way. If an off-the wall solution works and makes those who use it more satisfied with their jobs, then use it. Don't throw it out just because it's never been done before or because you didn't think of it first.

Don't answer an employee's suggestion with *"They* said it had to be done this way!" You're only passing the buck with an answer like that.

Instead of blindly following rules in each and every situation, start emphasizing the skills of your employees. To get peak performance for peak profits in your company, follow these eight guidelines:

1. Give a person a job to do and let him do it.

2. Urge your employee to use her skill, her initiative, and her ingenuity to beat your established standards.

3. Offer him security in return for his knowledge when he translates his know-how into skills on the job for you.

4. Get her to set up her own work goals and establish her own standards of performance.

5. Let him work in his own style if it doesn't interfere with the performance of others.

6. Set up a system to test an employee for his or her maximum potential.

7. Let him tell you how and where he needs to improve.

8. Let her recommend ways of improving work methods on her job.

"I'm not interested in methods—I'm interested in results!" said General George S. Patton, famed commander of World War II. "If you want to win, you've got to use skill, guts, determination, perseverance, initiative, ingenuity, and a dozen other fine qualities of leadership. But above all—you've got to throw away the rulebook!"

And General Patton's results speak for themselves. While other generals on both sides were still fighting by the rulebook of World War I, General Patton was writing a new one! When he fought, the so-called rules of conventional warfare went flying out the window.

He wrote his own rules and won; so can you!

SOLUTIONS: HOW TO USE AN SOP TO PREVENT PROBLEMS

One of the biggest headaches your subordinate managers and executives have is how to know which matters should be given to you for a final decision and which ones they can handle for themselves.

Of course, a good SOP (Standing—not *Standard*—Operating Procedure) will take care of many of those questions for them. An

SOP could vary in size from a few pages to a thick volume with hundreds of pages. Just remember that the thicker the SOP is, the greater will be the reader's resistance.

"A good SOP will solve most of your problems on the production line," says Walter Parks, manager of an automobile assembly plant in St. Louis. "It'll cover the operation and maintenance of most of your machinery. It encompasses most of the detailed day-to-day operation of your company, and that's as it should be.

"Of course, it won't answer all of your subordinates' questions nor will it solve all their problems. But I've found that the biggest question my foremen and supervisors have is always *should the boss know about this?* A good SOP will answer that question for them.

"If you're the boss, and if all the correspondence and paperwork falls on your back, as it does on mine, then *your SOP must let your immediate subordinates know what papers you must see and what correspondence you personally have to sign.* When they know that, then they'll also know automatically *what you don't have to see and what you don't have to sign.*

"To give guidance to my people in these two touchy areas, I put out this little memo which I call, 'Keep the Boss Informed.' Each department and section head has a copy of it on his or her desk. Each supervisor carries a copy in his pocket."

KEEP THE BOSS INFORMED

I want the following matters brought to my personal attention at once.

1. Any *important* subject that will require some *immediate action* on my part which is not specifically covered in some previously published policy or directive.

2. Letters of disapproval of any sort from my superiors.

3. Any and all errors, irregularities, or deficiencies in this organization's operation that have been pointed out by my superiors.

4. Any letters or reports that indicate neglect or dereliction of duty on the part of anyone in this company, or that carry even the slightest hint of criticism, censure, or reprimand.

5. Written appeals made by any subordinate about decisions that I or my immediate staff or anyone else in management has made.

6. Any subject that would injure the good name or reputation of the company.

7. Any *serious* accidents or incidents, on or off duty, which involve company personnel.

8. Any reports of financial irregularities or discrepancies or any shortage of property or materials.

The following matters will be sent to me for my personal action and/or my personal signature.

1. Any nonroutine letter or report that contains a request or a recommendation to be made to my superiors.

2. Letters or certificates of commendation, award, or appreciation that are to be given to any employee.

3. Any letter or report that will cast a shadow of doubt on the good name or reputation of any person or any department.

4. Letters of disapproval or negative replies on requests or suggestions from subordinates.

5. Any letter that contains the slightest hint of criticism, censure, or reprimand.

6. Letters or reports to be sent to any governmental agency.

7. Letters and reports that have to do with future planning.

8. Any letters and reports of *exceptional or outstanding information* not specifically covered in this memorandum.

"This isn't a cure-all," Walter says, "but when people know exactly what matters I want to know about, and specifically which papers to route through my office, it answers ninety-five percent of their questions. It speeds up their work and my desk is kept comparatively clean and clear, too."

I've seen a lot of SOPs in my time, both bad and good—short and long—simple and complicated. I've never seen a better one (or a shorter one) than Walter's, and I thank him for allowing me to use it in this book.

SOLUTIONS: THE DOCTRINE OF COMPLETED STAFF WORK

The Doctrine of Completed Staff Work is in a sense an SOP in itself.

An experienced executive or manager thinks his way carefully through each problem that his boss hands him to solve. He decides upon a definite line of procedure to follow. He determines what information he needs and which of his associates he needs to help gather it. He considers every possible angle and the viewpoints of all interested individuals before he reaches a final decision.

That's how an experienced executive or manager works. However, a young and inexperienced junior executive won't be able to do this so easily or so quickly. The following will be of great help to him, as well as to the experienced executive or manager.

DOCTRINE OF COMPLETED STAFF WORK

1. Completed staff work is the study of a problem and the presentation of a solution by an executive, a manager, a foreman, or anyone in the management chain of authority, in such a form that all that remains to be done on the part of the CEO is to indicate his approval or disapproval of the *completed action*. The words "completed action" are emphasized because the more difficult the problem is, the greater the tendency to present the problem to the CEO in piecemeal fashion. However, it is your duty to work out those details. You should not consult your chief in the determination of those details, no matter how perplexing they may be. You may and you should consult other managers or executives who can help you. Whether it involves the pronouncement of a new policy or affects an established one, the end product should be worked out in finished form, when presented to the chief for approval or disapproval.

2. This impulse that often arises in the inexperienced manager to ask the CEO what to do occurs more often when the problem is extremely difficult. This impulse is accompanied by a feeling of men-

tal frustration. While it is easy to ask the boss what to do, and it appears to be easy for him to answer, resist that impulse. It is your job to advise your boss what he ought to do, not to ask him what you ought to do. He needs answers, not questions. Your job is to study, write, restudy, and rewrite until you have worked out a single proposed action—the best one of all that you have considered. Your chief will simply approve or disapprove.

3. Do not worry your boss with long explanations and memoranda. Writing a memorandum to your chief does not constitute completed staff work, but writing a memorandum for him to send to someone else does. Your views should be placed before him in finished form so that he can make them his views simply by signing his name. In most instances, completed staff work results in a single document prepared for the signature of your chief, without accompanying comment. If the proper result is reached, the chief will usually recognize it at once. If he wants any further comment or explanation, he will ask you for it.

4. The theory of completed staff work does not preclude a "rough draft," but the rough draft must not be a half-baked idea. It must be complete in every respect except for the requisite number of copies and need not be so neat as a finished product. But a rough draft must not be used as an excuse for shifting the burden of formulating the action to your chief.

5. The "completed staff work" theory may result in more work for the subordinate executive or manager. But this is as it should be. Further, it accomplishes two things:

✔ The chief is protected from incomplete ideas, voluminous memoranda, and immature oral presentations.

✔ The subordinate executive or manager who has a real idea to sell is enabled more readily to find a market.

6. When you have finished your "completed staff work" the final test is this: If you were the chief, would you be willing to sign the paper you have prepared and stake your professional reputation on its being right? If your answer is in the negative, take it back and work it over again, because it is not yet "completed staff work."

SOLVING SUPERVISORY PROBLEMS

SOLUTIONS: HOW TO CORRECT AN EMPLOYEE'S MISTAKES WITHOUT CRITICIZING

"I used to run my department when I was a foreman like a cop hand- ing out traffic tickets," Dick Barnes, the production superintendent of a large Atlanta plant, told me. "I'd been given the idea by a tough old supervisor who was my first boss that I had to keep on every- body's tail every minute of the day to keep them working.

"Well, I ended up in the hospital for three weeks on a Sippy diet—a glass of Half and Half every hour on the hour and nothing but amphojel in between. In less than a week I was trying to run that hospital ward like my own department in the factory. I was raising the dickens with everyone and chewing out every person in sight. When they didn't listen to me or pay any attention to what I said, I got even madder at all of them.

"At my last consultation before I was discharged, my doctor said, 'You're giving yourself your own ulcers, Dick; your employees didn't give them to you. Neither did your boss or your job. Let me give you a little tip. Ease up, my friend, ease up. Live and let live. You'll enjoy life a lot more.'

"Well, I did as the doctor said. I had to, for I was giving myself a heart flutter as well as ulcers. That was over four years ago. I haven't had an ulcer attack and my heart hasn't skipped a beat since then.

"And, incidentally, I'm no longer a department foreman as I was back then. Since my change of attitude toward myself and others, I've been promoted to the production superintendent in charge of all manufacturing in the plant."

If you're having the same sort of problems Dick Barnes was having, let me give you the sixteen specific steps he gave me to correct an employee's mistakes without criticism or without turning it into a bigger problem—either for the employee or for yourself.

1. Call attention to a person's mistakes indirectly. (If you do this, you'll find out that you can do away with the requirement for a formal counseling session in 95 percent of your problem cases.)

2. First find out all the pertinent facts bearing on the problem.

3. Decide whether or not a formal counseling session is necessary.

4. If you decide that it is necessary, then pick the proper time and the proper place.

5. Never lose your temper with an employee when you are correcting his or her mistakes. Be objective, not subjective, about the problem.

6. Always begin with sincere praise and honest appreciation for the person's work.

7. Take your own inventory as well as the employee's. Explain how you've made the same sort of mistake in the past yourself.

8. Give your employee plenty of chance to talk and explain his or her actions.

9. Weigh all the evidence and the facts carefully. Do not, under any circumstances, jump to conclusions.

10. If punishment is warranted, then fit it to both the mistake and to the individual being punished.

11. Let a person select his own punishment. He'll usually be much tougher on himself than you are. Then when you reduce the "sentence," he'll be grateful to you for being so kind.

12. Close your interview with sincere praise and honest appreciation for his or her work.

13. Praise every improvement, even the slightest one.

14. Give your employee a high reputation to live up to.

15. Follow up with a second interview—if necessary.

16. Don't correct a person's mistakes too often. You're probably nagging, not correcting the person, when you do that.

SOLUTIONS: HOW TO SUCCESSFULLY HANDLE EMPLOYEE COMPLAINTS

Do you want your people to do their best for you? *Then let them come to you with their gripes and complaints.* When you do that, you'll be able to keep potential problem workers from becoming recalcitrant and bitter troublemakers.

Not long ago I was given permission by a large industrial company in Orlando, Florida, to interview some of its employees to find out why they had voted against unionizing the plant.

"How come?" I asked. "Is it because they pay higher wages than union plants? Do they offer you better benefits?"

"It's because they treat us like human beings, not robots," one man said. "They listen to our problems. They pay attention to our complaints."

"That's right," a woman spoke up. "That's the main reason, I think. Management listens to what we have to say and they do something about it. They treat us as if we're important members of the company—not just pieces of the machinery. I worked for a rubber factory before I came here and I was never treated as decently as I am now. Just the opposite, in fact, and I was in the union back there."

That was the general consensus of opinion. The employees didn't need a union because management already had a good grievance procedure. They helped the employees solve their problems. They listened to their people. They paid attention to their gripes and complaints.

Now let me give you the twelve specific guidelines the Orlando company's management gave me so you can use them to handle your employees' complaints quickly, easily, and successfully:

1. ***Make it easy for them to come to you***. You don't have to be overly chummy, but you should not be cold and distant either. The most important thing is to relieve your subordinates' fears that their complaints might antagonize you and create bigger problems for them than they already have.

2. ***Get rid of red tape***. Don't clutter up your grievance procedure with cumbersome rules and regulations that defeat your purpose. Keep it plain and simple. You want to get to the problem and its solution in the least amount of time possible. A good way to do this is to keep your door open at all times to your employees.

3. ***Explain your grievance procedure to everyone***. Keeping your door open does no good unless your employees know why it's open. Pass the word along, let them all know, keep everyone informed. State clearly and precisely how an employee should present a complaint and spell out what will happen when he or she does. Explain your procedure, step by step, so that everyone will understand it clearly.

4. ***Help a person voice her complaint***. Sometimes an employee may not be skilled in putting her grievance into words. If she feels that the successful correction of her problem will depend upon her verbal ability, she may give up even before she starts. Then she'll bottle up her discontent inside where it will fester and continue to grow into an open sore.

5. ***Always grant a hearing to an employee with a complaint***. No matter how trivial his complaint might sound to you, it's important to him. So always give your employee the chance to air his gripe and get it off his chest.

6. ***Practice patience***. I know that you are busy as an employer or a manager and have many things to do. But be patient; hear the person out. If you don't, the next time you hear him, it could well be at a formal arbitration hearing. Then you'll have to listen whether you want to or not, and it'll be much more expensive and time consuming.

7. ***Ask her what she wants you to do***. Here's how you can turn a complaint into a benefit for you. Just ask, "What would you

like me to do to help?" I've had people respond by saying, "I guess nothing, sir. I just wanted someone to hear my side of it. You've done that, so I'm satisfied."

Take it from me, this one question on your part will do more to oil the rusty relationships between management and labor than any other strategy that you might use.

8. ***Don't make hasty or biased decisions***. Make your decisions with the impartiality of a judge, not the biased view of management. Don't make hasty or snap judgments. If you need more time to get more information, take it. A wise decision is more important than a hasty one.

9. ***Get all the facts first***. Sometimes you will need to hear someone else's side of the story first before you can make your decision. If this is necessary to get all the facts, do so, no matter how much time it takes.

10. ***Let the employee know what your decision is.*** Once you've made your decision, let the person know what it is. Tell him yourself. Call him back to your office if need be to explain how you've decided to help him solve his problem. Don't pass the word to him via your clerk or secretary. Then he'll know for sure that you weren't really interested in his case after all.

11. ***Double-check your results***. Later on, check back with your employee to make sure her grievance has been taken care of to her complete satisfaction. Follow up and she will know that you really are interested in her welfare.

12. ***Be concerned***. There's not much point in paying attention to a person and listening to his complaint unless you honestly do care, unless you really want to help, unless you won't feel right until you do. I can't tell you how to work this step. It has to come from deep down inside of you.

SOLUTIONS: HOW TO ASK THE RIGHT QUESTIONS AND LISTEN TO THE ANSWERS

"If you want to get accurate and reliable information from your employees to find out what's really going on in your organization, you must learn to ask questions, questions, and still more questions," says Sandra Butler, an employee relations counselor.

"Never dominate the conversation by doing all the talking yourself if you want to find out where your people stand on a certain point. You must ask questions and then listen to the answers. To get more information, ask another question when the person stops talking. Just prime the pump; let him work the handle."

The following six-point checklist will help you ask questions that get reliable answers:

✔ *Your questions should have a specific purpose*. One question might be used to emphasize a major point, another to stimulate thought, and still another to arouse interest.

✔ *Your questions should be easily understood by everyone*. They should be phrased in words that are familiar to all your employees. If your question creates another question in your listener's mind, it's useless.

✔ *Your question must emphasize only one point at a time*. Avoid asking two questions in one or asking a question in such a way that other questions are needed to get the information you want. The words "This one thing I do" are as valid today as when the Apostle Paul wrote them to the Philippians almost 2,000 years ago.

✔ *Your question should ask for a definite answer*. Don't let your subordinates bluff you or get away with vague, non-specific answers that tell you nothing. Ask your questions in such a way that definite answers are required, and don't give up until you get them.

✔ *Your question should discourage guessing*. Never word your question in such a way that your listener can guess at an answer to satisfy you. His answer should be based on facts, not fancy. There'll be times when you want a person's candid opinion, but subjective thinking has to be based on objective facts.

✔ *The best question always asks "Why?"* The why can be spoken or implied, but it should always be there. Too many managers are satisfied with an answer of yes or no—even when that answer tells them nothing. If a person says yes, ask him why. If he says no, ask him why. That little three-letter word is one of the best ways to get accurate information from your employees and find out what's really going on in your organization.

Do you want to find out what's going on in your own organization? Then listen to your subordinates with an open mind. Do you want your people to respect you? Let them talk to you about their personal problems, their worries, and their fears. Do you want an employee to level with you—to tell you the whole truth? Then give him the courtesy of listening to what he has to say. *Listening carefully and attentively to what a person says is one of the highest compliments you can pay to anyone.* Here are ten techniques you can use to improve your listening abilities:

1. *Give your wholehearted attention to the person.* Listening with everything you have means putting aside your own interests, preoccupations, and problems—at least temporarily. For those few moments, concentrate 100 percent on what the other person is saying. Focus all your attention on him.

2. *Really work at listening.* Listening is hard work. When you listen intently, your heartbeat quickens and your blood circulates faster. You will know if you're really working at listening to the other person or just faking it.

3. *Show an interest in what the speaker is saying.* Look directly at the person. Establish eye contact and hold it. Show by your alert bearing and intense facial expression that you are concerned with what he's saying. Above all, don't fiddle with objects on your desk or clip your nails.

4. *Resist distractions.* If the conversation takes place in your office, tell your secretary you don't want to be disturbed. Shut the door, cut off the telephone, turn off the radio. Give the speaker every chance to tell you what you need to know. If you don't, he might react the way I did once in a doctor's office.

We were receiving a final report from a high-priced neuro-surgeon about my wife's physical condition. He was interrupted three times by phone calls from his secretary. The fourth time the phone rang, I picked it up, and said, "The doctor is out. He won't be back for thirty minutes. Don't call again before two-thir-ty!"

5. **Show patience**. Patience is a matter of listening silently until the person has stopped speaking. The tempo of his thinking may be slower than yours, so understand why he's slower in express-ing himself than you are.

6. **Keep an open mind**. Remember that you're listening to gain information. If her ideas don't coincide with yours, it doesn't mean you're right and she's wrong. Wise managers of large, successful companies will be quick to tell you that most innovations in business and industry come from rank-and-file workers.

7. **Listen for ideas.** A good listener watches for ideas, concepts, and principles. A poor listener gets lost in details. If an employee has an idea to speed up production and eliminate waste, keep your eye on that point. Don't fret if you can't remember all the details by heart. That can all be worked out later.

8. **Judge the content, not the delivery**. Don't get upset over a person's style of delivery. You should be interested only in finding out what he knows. I once worked for a man who'd been a college English professor. That bothered me a great deal until one day he said, "I'm not grading you on your grammar, sentence struc-ture, or choice of words, Jim. I'm only interested in *what* you're telling me, not *how* you're saying it."

9. **Hold your fire.** Many times a listener spends his time try-ing to figure out how to rebut the speaker rather than listening to what's being said. You might learn something new and profitable if you teach your ego to "hold its breath."

10. **Learn to listen between the lines**. Lots of times you can learn more by what the other person doesn't say than by what he does. You must use your eyes as well as your ears to listen.

SOLUTIONS: HOW TO TURN AN ANGRY EMPLOYEE INTO A HAPPY ONE

As I just discussed in the last solution, learning to ask good questions and listening to employees' answers could help you solve your problems with people. I gave you a six-point checklist for asking questions that would get reliable answers. And I gave you ten techniques you could use to improve your listening skills.

Now, I want to show you how you can use this same listening skill to turn an angry employee into a happy and satisfied one.

I learned this technique from a master in the business, Roy Feldman, a top employee relations manager. Here, in his own words, is how he does it:

"When an angry employee comes through my door with a complaint, I handle him like a VIP," Roy says. "I treat him as if he were the president of the company or a majority stockholder. I have him sit down. I make him comfortable, offer him a cup of coffee. I do everything I can to put him completely at ease.

"These actions alone take some of the fire out of him. Then after he's settled down in his easy chair with a cup of coffee, I ask him to tell me his story. I tell him I want to hear it all from beginning to end. Then I listen to what he says without interrupting him or saying a single word. That's the first thing he wants—someone who will listen to him—someone who will lend a sympathetic ear to his troubles.

"When he's all through, I tell him I can sure understand how he feels. I say that if I were in his position, if the situation were reversed, I'd no doubt feel the same way he does.

"Now I've taken a lot of the steam out of him simply by listening to him and by telling him I understand how he feels. He wasn't prepared for that at all, so he calms down even more. Instead of finding that I'm his enemy, he suddenly finds that I'm his friend; I'm on his side. He came in prepared to do battle with me, but now he finds he has no one to fight!

"Next I ask him what he wants me to do about his complaint. This really floors him because most of the time a manager doesn't *ask* his employee what he can do for him. Instead, he *tells* him what he's going to do. But we don't run our employee relations program that way. We never tell an employee with a complaint what we're going to do—*we ask him what he wants us to do for him.*

"I've had people look at me in astonishment and say, 'Gee, Mr. Feldman, I honestly don't know. I hadn't thought about that. I just wanted someone to listen to my side of the story for a change. You've done that so that's enough. I'm satisfied.'

"Sometimes they do tell me what they want me to do. Ninety-five times out of a hundred, I find that they ask for far less that I would've offered. Then when I give them more than they've asked for, they are really impressed with the generosity of both management and the company.

"Either way, when they leave, they're fully satisfied. In both cases, they supplied themselves with their own answers, so they're bound to be happy with the end results.

"Actually, my job is easy. All I do is listen. Then I ask what he wants me to do. Then I help him get what he wants."

COMMUNICATING WITH YOUR STAFF

"A speaker doesn't always put everything he's thinking into words,"
Dr. Janet Bradford, a clinical psychologist, says. "In fact, university
studies show that over ninety percent of any message is transmitted
nonverbally. That being so, it becomes extremely important not only
to know how to use body language yourself, but also to be able to
read another person's body signals."

Nonverbal communication involves much less deception than
spoken language. We find it easier to lie with words than with our
bodies. For instance, have you ever tried to keep your hands still, or
keep from biting your lips, or not sighing when you were extremely
nervous or worried about something? Impossible, wasn't it? No matter what you said, your body told others what you were really feeling.

When one of your subordinates is talking with you, look at his
face first to see if his expression goes with what he is saying. Then
listen to the tone of his voice to see if you can find a hidden meaning somewhere. Finally, listen to his spoken words to see if they go
with his body signals.

Here are some clues that can help you to understand body language when you're listening to an employee:

1. *Eyes*. No matter what her mouth says, her eyes will tell you what she's really thinking. If the pupils widen, then she likes what she's heard. You've made her feel good by what you've said. If her pupils contract, just the opposite is true. She's heard something she dislikes. If her eyes narrow, you've told her something she doesn't believe or she feels she has cause not to trust you or what you say.

2. *Eyebrows*. If he lifts one eyebrow, you've told him something he doesn't believe or that he thinks is impossible. Lifting both eyebrows indicates surprise at what you've said.

3. *Mouth*. A broad smile is a sign of real happiness and joy. But watch out for a smile that shows only the upper teeth. It's just a polite smile or one that shows that the person is really uncomfortable with you.

4. *Nose and ears*. If he rubs his nose or tugs at his ear while saying he understands, it mean's he's puzzled by what you're saying and probably has no idea what you want him to do.

5. *Forehead*. If she wrinkles her forehead downward in a frown, it means she's puzzled or she doesn't like what you've told her. If she wrinkles her forehead upward, it indicates surprise at what she's just heard.

6. *Shoulders*. When a person shrugs his shoulders, it usually means he's completely indifferent. He doesn't give a hoot for what you're saying or what you want.

7. *Fingers*. Drumming or tapping his fingers on the arm of his chair or the top of his desk indicates either nervousness or impatience.

8. *Arms*. If she clasps her arms across her chest, it usually means she's trying to isolate herself from others, or that she's actually afraid of you and is trying to protect herself.

Now here are two techniques you can use to project the power of your personality without ever saying a single word:

The Steepling Technique.

Smart people who want to project the power of their personalities often make a steeple with their hands. Watch a group of people during a business meeting. As the boss listens to a subordinate's suggestion, she will often steeple. This shows she is seriously thinking about what the other person is saying. As her thoughts become deeper and more profound, she may steeple in a higher and higher position until the steeple nearly hides her face.

Medical doctors, psychiatrists, and psychologists are all avid steeplers. The implication is that they are deep thinkers and extremely intelligent and important people. Use the steepling technique and people will draw the same conclusions about you.

Invading another person's territory with your eyes.

Powerful people are accustomed to staring down other individuals as a way of invading their territory. Usually, if the boss stares at an employee, the employee will lower his eyes and only glance up now and then to sneak a quick look at his superior.

There's a simple trick to this staring technique. *Never, never look directly into the other person's eyes.* Instead, pick a spot in the middle of his forehead just above the level of his eyebrows. Keep your eyes glued to that one spot and no one will ever be able to stare you down. Eventually, the other person will have no choice but to lower his gaze.

Here are five final tips on projecting the power of your personality:

1. ***Don't smile unless you are genuinely happy.*** This doesn't mean you have to walk around with a frown on your face. It means exactly what it says. Don't smile unless you are really happy. A neutral facial expression best conceals your inner feelings.

2. ***Don't allow people to interrupt you.*** If someone does interrupt you, even if it's your superior, simply say, "I'm sorry, but I wasn't finished," and then resume speaking at once where you were cut off. This is enough to stop the other person dead in his tracks unless he is abnormally obtuse.

3. *Don't restrain your body gestures*. If you need to use your hands or arms to make a point, do so. The only thing to avoid is pointing your finger at someone as if you were accusing him of some wrong. This turns everyone off completely.

4. *Look people straight in the eye*. As I said earlier, the trick to this is staring at a spot in the middle of the forehead just above the eyebrows. This is the most effective technique you can use to make the other person back off. If he's trying to argue with you, saying nothing but staring at him this way will cause him to become nervous and flustered. You can make your point without ever saying a single word.

5. *Be completely relaxed*. I don't mean you should be sloppy about your dress or careless about your appearance. The key to being relaxed is self-confidence. If you know your job, you don't have to be nervous and filled with tension. You can relax and really enjoy your work.

SOLUTIONS: HOW TO KEEP PEOPLE INFORMED AND PREVENT PERSONNEL PROBLEMS

"Most personnel problems come from employees not having enough information about what management has done and why," says Barry Hunter, production superintendent for a California steel corporation. "It's important that you let people know *what* you are going to do, *when, why,* and *how,* especially if your actions are going to affect them.

"For instance, just last week, one of our production employees was upset because it seemed as if a newer man had been promoted ahead of him. So he filed a grievance with his shop steward and in less than twenty-four hours he received a full explanation that satisfied him.

"The man who'd been promoted had joined the company after Hank had, but before that he'd worked for more than six years for a company we'd bought out. One of the conditions of that purchase was that all members of the company would be credited for the years they'd worked there. As it turned out, the man who was promoted had two years seniority on Hank.

"Hank's complaint would never have been filed if he'd been given the proper information in the first place. That was my fault; I didn't pass the word along the way I should've. You can bet that everybody in the place has the full story now."

There's no reason for you to run your organization in such a way that your people have to ask you questions like that. *Every single employee of yours has the basic right to information on actions and decisions that affect them.* Nobody should have to work and think in the dark.

They should be told the *why* and the *wherefore* of whatever they are expected to do, as well as the *what* and the *how.* Their efficiency, morale, confidence, and enthusiasm will depend largely on how well you do that.

If you consistently brush off your subordinates, not keeping them properly informed, then you are doomed to work in an information vacuum yourself. Here are some techniques that you can use to keep people properly informed:

Let people know exactly where they stand with you.

"Most people worry about what the boss thinks of them and the way they do their job, especially when he stands there and watches them work without saying a single word," says Dan Baker, production supervisor with a California chemical company. "Don't you? Well, your subordinates are no different than you are.

"I don't make my people guess. I don't play games with them. I tell them the truth; I level with them. If I think a person isn't doing his job properly, I tell him so. But if he's doing a good job, I let him know that, too. I find I can get even better results when I keep my people informed about their progress on the job."

Let them know of any changes that will affect them.

Not only should you let people know how they're doing on the job, you should also *keep them informed of any changes that will affect them.* You don't have to reveal company secrets, but you do have a moral obligation to let people know about any planned changes that will affect their job security, their income, or their future. It's one way you can show your concern for your employees' welfare.

For instance, if changes in your company will create a new position in a department other than your own for which one of your people is qualified, tell her about it. She's entitled to the chance to better herself.

You might handicap your operation temporarily by losing a good worker, but you'll benefit in the long run. And if she doesn't get the job, at least she'll be grateful to you for having given her the chance to try for it. If she misses, she'll appreciate your thoughtfulness and do an even better job for you than before.

Also let them know of any changes that will not affect them.

Just as it's important to let people know when certain changes *are* going to affect them, it's just as important—in fact, sometimes more so—to let them know when contemplated changes are *not* going to affect them. Here's a glaring example of how things can go wrong when you fail to follow this simple rule:

"Seemingly out of a clear blue sky last summer we started getting all sorts of complaints from our production employees," says Betty Anderson, the industrial relations director for a large electrical appliance manufacturer in Chicago. "They grumbled about poor lighting, bad ventilation, excessive heat, noise, and so on. As each problem was satisfactorily resolved, they'd come up with still another one.

"This was not like our people at all, for we've always enjoyed extremely cordial relations with our employees, so I called in one of the women who's been with us a long time to see if I could find out what was really at the bottom of all these sudden complaints.

"Well, I found out their real problem was the fear they were going to be the victims of automation and lose their jobs. You see, we'd had a professional leasing firm in to survey our plant with the idea of selling the building to them and then renting it back on a long-term lease. That way we could free up a lot of capital for expansion purposes that was tied up in our physical plant.

"But the sudden and unexplained appearance of a lot of strangers with pencils and notebooks had aroused our employees' suspicions. They were dead certain they were going to be replaced with more machines. Once the reason for all the strangers was explained, the complaints stopped."

You can get this same kind of static, too, unless you try to prevent such misunderstandings by keeping your people fully informed. When things do go wrong, remember that you can often quickly clear the air by asking your employees a few well-placed questions.

SOLUTIONS: HOW TO HAVE YOUR STAFF KEEP YOU INFORMED

I have told you why it is so important for you to keep your staff informed to keep problems from happening, but communication is a two-way street. The first part consists of keeping your staff well informed and up to date. The second part is letting your employees tell you what's going on in your own organization. And that's the part I want to discuss with you now.

Here is a simple example of why it is so important for an employee to keep the boss informed. In the small town of Indiatlantic on the east coast of Florida, there is a cute little restaurant named the *Blueberry Muffin*. The food is outstanding and the service is superb. The only drawback is that the seating capacity is somewhat limited, so there's always a long line of people waiting for a table.

In spite of our usually having to wait, my companion and I often eat breakfast there since the food is so tasty and the atmosphere so friendly and cordial.

One morning we had ham, scrambled eggs, grits, and a blueberry muffin. Unfortunately, the ham was not the best that day.

As usually happens in any good restaurant, the waitress came to ask if everything was all right. "Well, to tell you the truth, Rose," I said, "the ham wasn't up to par this morning. It had a great deal of gristle in it and it was very tough."

"Oh, I'm ever so sorry," the waitress said, and I thought, well, that's the end of that, but it wasn't.

In less than two minutes, the owner of the restaurant, Bill Kokotis, was standing by our table. "Rose tells me you had a problem with the ham this morning," he said. "Please tell me what was wrong."

I repeated what I had already told Rose, and Bill said, "I'm so sorry. I tell the cook not to serve ham when it gets too close to the end to get a good cut, but I guess I'll have to remind him again. Let me get you some more."

"No, Bill, we've had enough and we're ready to go, but thanks anyway," I said.

A few moments later Rose handed me the check and we discovered that the ham had been taken off our bill. By letting her boss know the situation, she kept him informed about a customer's dissatisfaction. And by not charging us for the ham, Bill ensured that he would keep us as steady, satisfied customers.

Now, just like Bill Kokotis, wouldn't you want to know what's going on in your own organization—whether it's a section, a department, or the entire company? *Then listen to your subordinates with an open mind.* Pay attention to what they want to tell you. *Listen, listen, and then listen some more.* You'll be sure to find out what's actually going on in your own organization. And you'll be certain to benefit by doing so.

MOTIVATING EMPLOYEES

SOLUTIONS: HOW TO MAKE YOUR EMPLOYEES FEEL THEY'RE PART OF THE TEAM

The other morning I read in the newspaper how the employees of one of the big-three automobile manufacturers stood and cheered as the first new model rolled off the assembly line. A company executive said they had instituted a new management-employee program that stressed cooperation and teamwork. The company had used 135 employee suggestions to improve their new model car. That made the employees feel that they were part of the team, not just assembly-line workers.

One of the strongest psychological drives a person has is the desire to belong, to have identification with a group. When you give him that identification as a team member, you'll motivate him to do his best for you.

When she knows that she's wanted and her work is appreciated by the members of her group, when she knows that her efforts are contributing to the achievement of a common goal, then she becomes proud of herself, proud of her group, proud of her superiors, and proud of her company. She'll be motivated to be a loyal team member.

Here is a specific example: A Michigan manufacturer of car mirrors for the automobile industry was forced to turn to its employees and solicit their help and teamwork because of financial problems. But even when the financial position of the company improved, the chief executive officer was wise enough to see the advantages of retaining the new system.

One of the biggest Detroit customers of this company had presented an ultimatum: Either the company had to lower its prices or the buyer would go somewhere else to find a new supplier of car mirrors.

A machine operator on the assembly line knew a method that would reduce his crew of five people to four and help save the company money. But he hesitated to offer his idea to the company management when the employees were asked for help in reducing costs. He didn't want to lose his own job and he didn't want to cause one of his co-workers to lose their job either.

So he approached management this way. He said he would give his cost-cutting idea to the company if they would promise that no one would lose his or her job as a result. The company management agreed to this condition. They also extended the same guarantee to any employee who could come up with suggestions on how to reduce production costs. Here are the benefits that everyone gained:

✔ Every employee can receive as high a pay raise as his cost-cutting idea will pay for.

✔ Every employee gets monthly bonus checks that can go as high as 20 percent of her base pay.

✔ The company is prospering. Employment has almost doubled since this program was started.

✔ The company's main product sells for 15 percent less than it did before in spite of inflation.

Employees are happy and satisfied. They have learned, and so has management, that everyone benefits when they all work together as one big team toward a common goal.

Here is another example showing how a lack of teamwork can cause a loss of profit. "We were going in the red in our Kansas City plant month after month," Claude Vance told me. "I was getting scared. After all, plant managers don't keep their jobs for long that way. Big corporations like ours don't hold still for losses in their branch plants. It's either produce and make a profit, or get out for someone who can!

"The scrap and waste in our building departments was terrible. We were hauling more out the back door to the city dump than we could sell out the front door.

"I kept after my production superintendent and the general foremen to cut down on this scrap and waste, but I was getting nowhere. Everyone was too busy blaming the other fellow to clean up his own mess. I had them giving me daily scrap reports, weekly scrap reports, and monthly scrap reports! Complete waste of time and effort.

"When I tried to check them out, I'd find that if Smith's report was low one week, then Jones's would be high. The next week, if Smith and Jones were both low, then Brown's or Black's would be up, and so it went, on and on.

"All they were doing was passing the buck back and forth between them with employees physically trying to sneak scrap out of one department into another. Of course, the total amount of scrap going out the back door never did decrease.

"At last I saw what I was doing wrong. Instead of trying to find out *why* we had so much waste, I'd just been yelling at everyone to stop it. I had seven general foremen at each other's throat instead of cooperating and trying to help each other.

"Once we all got together, we were able to approach the problem with one common goal in mind, and we licked it. But it took a lot of cooperation, teamwork, and a mutual understanding of the other person's problems."

To sum up, teamwork is the key to the successful operation of any organization. It is one of the best tools a manager can use to get results. Teamwork must start at the top and work down to the last person to be truly effective. Each person must know where he fits in as a team member if you want him to give his utmost for the group effort.

Effective teamwork requires a high state of morale, esprit, discipline, and individual proficiency. At the same time, good teamwork promotes all these, and, in addition, it contributes to the total organizational efficiency.

In your emphasis of the efforts of the group as a whole, never neglect an individual's accomplishments. Always weigh and balance the two. The recognition of the individual and the final accomplishment of the group are both important.

When you give an individual the proper recognition, you'll help satisfy her needs for recognition and importance. By the same token, that person will also get a feeling of pride in her accomplishments as a member of the team.

SOLUTIONS: HOW TO USE COMPETITION TO GET SUPERIOR RESULTS

Desire is the first law of gain. And competition, or the effort to do better than someone else, grows out of that deep desire for gain. However, competition covers a much broader scope than gain alone.

Competition can masquerade under many disguises. When it erupts as jealousy or envy or greed for another person's talents, possessions, or position, it becomes unhealthy and an undesirable motivating force.

Competition properly used, however, produces leaders. A person can have education and intelligence, organizational ability, and be able to make sound and timely decisions, but unless that drive is sparked by the enthusiasm of a competitive spirit, the person will be of little use to you. Any business firm, company, or corporation worthy of its name always promotes competition among its employees.

Competition brings progress by encouraging the development of better products at better prices. It makes the customer the boss of the economy.

A competitor's ability should never be underestimated. The business graveyard is full of companies who figured the competition was stupid, shortsighted, or just plain lazy.

Competition makes life worth living. It keeps you alert and in peak condition. Without competition, you would find the race less interesting and victory less satisfying.

A competitor sometimes does more for you than does a friend. A friend is too polite to point out your weaknesses, but a competitor will take the trouble to advertise them for you.

You can use competition in four ways:

✔ Get a person to compete with himself—to beat his own record.

✔ Create competition between individuals.

✔ Establish competition between groups, for example, departments or sections.

✔ Promote competition with other companies or corporations.

Now here is the best technique I know of that you can use to spur competition in your organization: *Throw down a challenge to get results.*

"I consider my ability to arouse the competitive spirit in a person the greatest asset I have," says Earl Lane, a highly paid executive trouble-shooter for the Dominion Corporation.

"When one of our plants, which manufactures plastic parts for the rest of our corporation, was having trouble meeting its production quota, I was sent down there to find out why. The plant manager could give me no answer: neither could the production superintendent or his mill foreman. They all knew which department was at fault, but no one knew why.

"I was determined to find out for myself. I had to, for assembly lines in our other plants were bogged down for lack of parts. We were in a critical position, for some of our best customers—woolen and textile mills who use our parts in their big weaving looms—were threatening to cancel their business with us. I had to have an immediate solution to the problem, so I went right out on the production line to find the answer.

"'How many units did your shift produce today?' I asked the supervisor.

"'Three hundred,' was his answer.

"It was just about half his capacity. He knew it and so did I, but I said nothing more to him. Instead, I walked over to the mill department's bulletin board by the time clock. I tore a sheet of paper from my clipboard, tacked it up on the board and wrote 300 on it. Then I simply turned my back on the supervisor and left.

"When the next shift came in, some of the men called the new supervisor's attention to the 300 on the bulletin board. They wanted to know what it meant and so did he. Not only was he told what it stood for, but he was also informed by the outgoing shift supervisor that it couldn't be topped! *The first supervisor had already risen to the bait!*

"How wrong that day shift supervisor was," Earl went on to say. "When he came to work the next morning, he found the 300 had been crossed out and a new sheet of paper with a 500 on it was covering it up. *The second supervisor had also been hooked!*

"By the time I was ready to leave, that plant was exceeding its daily quota and was able to stockpile some of its production just in case a real emergency came along. Costwise, it has risen from the least efficient plant in our system to the top one during the past year, just from throwing down a challenge to get results!"

I know there are other techniques you could use to spur competition in your organization, not only inside your company, but with outside competitors as well, but throwing down a challenge can't be topped. When you use it, you'll gain these valuable benefits:

1. An increase in the working output of every employee from the bottom on up through the executive management level.

2. Increased production of a better quality product.

3. Employee initiative and enthusiasm.

4. Better quality products or better service to your customers. Competition acts as a spur to your organizational growth and progress.

5. Employee efficiency—competition makes the job and life worthwhile.

6. More money!

SOLUTIONS: HOW TO BUILD A SUPERIOR OPERATION— WITH ORDINARY PEOPLE

When you have a superior operation, you'll have increased organizational efficiency that runs from the front door to the back door; from your personnel and administrative sections through your production lines on out to your packing and shipping departments. And with peak performance throughout your place, you'll enjoy increased profits, too.

Jack Miller, the president of a highly successful, prominent Florida general contracting firm, and I discussed over lunch one day how he had been able to build a superior outfit with just ordinary people. Here's what Jack told me:

"I followed four basic principles to build my company. First, I accepted the fact that the superior outfit must be created from the ordinary and average run of people. Second, I used the principle that all my employees must want to do what I want them to do. Third, every single person in my company must be motivated to do his or her level best. And fourth, the superior outfit is the one that is better than any other in the field in all aspects."

Let's discuss each of those precepts, starting with the one that *the superior outfit must be created from the average and ordinary run of people.* Do you accept this idea? It's true, isn't it? Ever hear a retired military man reminisce about his years in service? He's quite a dreamer, really. "Why, if I could have that first sergeant I had in France in World War II," he says. "And if I had that young captain I met in Korea; and that operations officer who served with me in Vietnam. If I could just have all those guys together at one time, what an outfit I could build!"

Well, we just don't have the opportunity to be that selective in picking our personnel. Usually, to get employees, you put an ad in the paper that says, in essence, "Wanted: good people . . . good wages . . ." and depending upon how badly you need employees and how tight the labor market is, you're going to get the run of the mill—from the top to the bottom—just plain ordinary people. No Einsteins, no Von Brauns, no geniuses. Just people named Smith and Brown and Jones—and Van Fleet and Van der Zee, along with Sloditski and Murphy and McClenahan. Maybe even some Wongs and Obayashis, too.

So creating a superior operation is basically the task of raising each employee's individual efforts to a level that is acceptable to you. Some will require more time and patience and attention than others. *But you have to start with those ordinary individuals.*

Second, many people think that motivation is the ability to get people to do what you want them to do. But that's not quite right. President Truman put it in a nutshell when he said, "Motivation is the ability to get people to *want* to do what you want them to do and to *like* doing it." The real art of motivation is to reach every person in your organization in such a way that each one will be stimulated to give you his peak performance at all times. When you can get your people in that frame of mind, you're well on your way to creating that superior outfit you want.

The third principle you can use to build a superior outfit with ordinary people is by *getting each man or woman—every single one of your employees—to do their level best for you at all times.*

"Whenever you see a company that's a leader in its field, you can be sure of one thing," says Barney Owens, personnel manager for an Illinois company. "They don't have any superhumans working for them. They have just plain, ordinary, average citizens; people just like you and me.

"How can I be so sure of that? Man alive, I look at applications for employment every single day of the week. I've interviewed hundreds, maybe thousands, of people since I've been in personnel work. Sure, our company is tops in its field, but we've got ordinary people working for us, too.

"How do we go about getting extraordinary results from these ordinary people? By getting every one of our employees to do their best at all times. That's how *we* do it, and that's how other top-notch companies do it, too. Our policy is *always do your best. You can't do more, and you shouldn't want to do less.* General Robert E. Lee said that more than a hundred years ago. It's still as true today as it was when he said it."

The last principle is that *the superior outfit is the one that is best in ALL THINGS.* One outfit like that was the Portland, Oregon Albina Shipyard in World War II. Here are some of the amazing facts about their record:

1. Albina operated on its own money and refused government financing of its military orders.

2. Morale among Albina workers was so high that absenteeism was only 2.95 percent—the lowest in the United States. (The industrial average at that time was 11 percent—nearly four times that of Albina!)

3. Albina workers subscribed a total per person for war bonds that was nine times greater than the total per person in other war plans.

4. Albina workers broke every subchaser building record.

5. Their athletic teams won every war industries sport championship.

6. Albina's flag carried four navy efficiency stars—the highly coveted Navy E for excellence—an honor earned by no other American shipyard.

7. Because of Albina's outstanding record, the United States government appointed it as an expediter for war materials for thirty-five other subchaser yards.

Secretary of the Navy Frank Knox said, "Albina has done more to improve the morale of the Navy than any other single influence since Pearl Harbor."

Let me conclude by saying that no outfit can be superior unless the boss is superior, too, and in Albina's case, the boss, L.R. Hussa, certainly fulfilled that requirement!

SOLUTIONS: HOW TO MAKE EVERY EMPLOYEE A SUPERIOR EMPLOYEE

You just learned how to build a superior outfit with ordinary people using four principles, one of which was that every person in your organization must be motivated to do his or her level best for you. Now I want to give you the secret you can use to ensure that all your employees will do that for you all the time.

The importance of motivation cannot be overemphasized. Andrew Carnegie, the steel magnate, who lived from 1835 to 1919, paid Charles Schwab a million dollars a year because of his ability to motivate people to do their best. And that was long before the inflated salaries of today's sports figures and corporation executives. Today, Charles Schwab's annual salary would no doubt be at least 10 or 12 million dollars.

Let's listen to what Charles Schwab himself had to say about his ability to motivate people: "I consider my ability to arouse enthusiasm in people the greatest asset I have. And the way to develop the best that is in a person is by appreciation and encouragement.

"There is nothing that will kill the ambitions of a person more quickly than criticism. So I never criticize anyone. I am anxious to praise, but loath to find fault. If I like something, I am always hearty in my approbation and lavish in my praise.

"I have yet to find the person who will not do better work and put forth greater effort under a spirit of approval and praise than he would ever do under a spirit of criticism."

That's what Charles Schwab always did. Praise instead of criticize. Is that what most bosses do? No, they do the exact opposite. If they don't like something, they raise the very devil about it. If they do like it, they say absolutely nothing. And then they wonder why they can't get the best out of their employees.

So if you want your employees to do their level best for you, then praise them. Tell them what a magnificent job they're doing for you, how much you need them, how you can't get along without them, how happy you are that they're in your organization.

We all hunger for a word of praise. We all need recognition and appreciation. No one is immune. As Mark Twain once said, "I could live for two months on one good compliment."

So be generous with your praise. Pass it around freely; the supply is limited only by you. Don't be stingy about passing out bouquets; they cost you nothing. Above all, never act as if you expect something in return for your praise. Don't pay a person a compliment as if you wanted a receipt for it.

Praise is the best way to make a person feel important. But criticism is the quickest way to destroy a person and make him your enemy. Nothing is more destructive to a person's pride and self-esteem than criticism. Listen to Carla Evans, a store manager for Fairfield Fashions in Orlando, Florida, as she tells why she uses praise instead of criticism with her employees:

"Some people say they find it hard to praise a person, but I disagree with that," Carla says. "It's actually easy to find something to compliment in a person and make her feel important. All you need do is look for something good about the individual instead of something bad.

"For instance, you can say, 'You really handled that difficult customer skillfully, Jane; that's really a top-notch idea, Fran; I sure appreciate your getting that report out ahead of time, Alice; thanks for staying late and getting those letters out yesterday, Mary.'

"See how easy it is to do? It all depends on what you're look-ing for. If you want to praise a person and make her feel more important, you can always find something to compliment her for. If you want to criticize her, you can always find something wrong, too. But I'd rather praise than criticize. I find it's a much better way to get my employees to do their best."

I agree with Carla. I never criticize anyone, either. I have enough character defects of my own to worry about without taking someone else's inventory. I do make helpful suggestions or show a person how to improve his work methods, but I do not use criticism to do that. I always go out of my way to praise a person, but I am extremely reluctant to find fault.

Here are five small words you can use to make a person feel important. *I am proud of you* are five of the most valuable and pow-erful words in the English language. You can use them any time on your employees, associates, friends, spouse, and your children.

Does this method work? It most certainly does. I'm not the only one to use it either. George Wheeler, vice president and general manager of a midwestern television station, uses it, too.

"I've never found any better words to use with my employees than *I'm proud of you,*" George says. "That's one of the highest compliments you can pay a person.

"When an employee does an exceptionally fine piece of work or turns in a terrific money-saving or cost-cutting idea, just to say 'Thanks' isn't enough. I go to him right in front of all the rest of my people, pat him on the back, and say 'Thanks a lot for what you did, Bill; *I'm real-ly proud of you.*' He'll work even harder for me from then on. So will everyone else. They all want some of that sweet syrup, too."

Praise instead of criticism will also work with your children. Don't criticize them if they bring home low grades from school. Do that and they'll go even lower. I know that for sure for I raised three of my own.

You can also use praise to correct mistakes.

Here's an example:

"Miss Jones, your typing is outstanding. You make very few errors and your work is clean and neat. Your spelling is exceptional-ly accurate. However, the change you made in this letter changes the exact meaning of what I wanted to say."

"Joe, you did outstanding work on this difficult project on such short notice. I know you were under a lot of pressure, but I've found one thing here I don't seem to understand. I wonder if you'd mind checking this measurement again for accuracy. It seems to me to be a little off. If it is, the whole thing might be thrown out of whack. Except for this one little point, though, your report was really terrific and I sure do appreciate your work on it."

"Tim, your report card really looks terrific this time. I'm really proud of your work. Your history grade is the only one that's down a little."

So always correct a person's mistakes by using praise. That way, you don't destroy his or her dignity and self-respect. You've let the person save face. I know it takes time, patience, and understanding to use this technique, but the end results are well worth the efforts expended.

All you have to do to prove it to yourself is to use praise with your employees. You'll be really happy with the results.

SOLUTIONS: HOW TO GET YOUR EMPLOYEES TO BACK YOU TO THE HILT

As a manager, an executive, or a supervisor, you are responsible for everything your employees do or fail to do. All too many managers are perfectly happy to take the credit when their subordinates are doing everything right, but extremely reluctant to take the blame when things go wrong.

But the door swings both ways. If you're willing to take credit for their good work, then you must also be willing to accept the blame for their mistakes. So when things go wrong, you must accept responsibility for what they have done and not allow others to chastise them. You must absorb their punishment for them.

The best way to do that is to use the "buffer technique" to protect them. When you do this, your subordinates will cooperate with you, support you, and back you to the hilt. Here's what the buffer technique is and how it works.

A company controller I know, Floyd Martin, was having all sorts of trouble with his subordinates. Late payrolls were an especially sore point with him, for they were a constantly recurring problem.

When different department heads would take him to task for this, Floyd would bark back testily, saying, "That's not my fault. I don't make up the blasted payrolls myself." Then he would pass the buck down to one of his subordinates. That person would then catch it from both Floyd and the complaining department head.

Floyd was discussing his situation with me one day and wanted to know if I had a solution he could use. "Floyd, you're taking the wrong approach to solving this problem," I said. "As long as you pass the blame down to someone else, you're going to continue having this difficulty. You're never going to solve your problem this way.

"But just as soon as you start accepting the responsibility for the mistakes of your subordinates and act as a buffer between them and those complaining department heads, you'll find that your people will back you to the hilt. They'll get the job done right and on time. When you protect them, they'll protect you."

Floyd was doubtful that this was the solution to his problem, but he decided to try it, more or less as a last resort. Naturally, this method worked for him just as I knew it would.

When you do this, you'll find people will go all out to keep mistakes from happening. When you keep them out of trouble, they are anxious to keep you out of trouble, too. The buffer technique, properly used, is a great persuader.

IMPROVING OVERALL PRODUCTIVITY

SOLUTIONS: TAKE RESPONSIBILITY FOR YOUR ACTIONS

Although you might have a great many outstanding leadership traits to help you qualify for a high-level executive position, there is one characteristic above all that you must possess or you'll never make it to the top. That is your willingness to take complete responsibility for your own actions.

As a manager or an executive in a company, you will no doubt be given the full power to decide upon a course of action—to give orders—to guide and correct the actions of others in your own department, section, or division.

And as a manager or executive, you must be willing to assume full responsibility for your own individual actions or for your failure to take action. You must also be willing to assume the full responsibility for all your organization does or fails to do—for its failures as well as for its successes.

To you, then, will go either the glory or the blame. If it's glory, be prompt in passing the credit and the commendations on down to your subordinates. But you must accept the blame all by yourself.

Of course, you'll be expected to take the proper corrective action to remedy a bad situation, but you, and you alone, have to accept full responsibility for the mistakes of your subordinates. As an executive or a manager, you cannot get off the hook by saying, "But I told him to do it this way. It's not my fault that he didn't." This will never be accepted as an explanation for failure by your superiors. It will be regarded only as an excuse. So don't try to evade the responsibility for failure by passing the buck to someone else. If you do that, your superiors will see through your flimsy facade at once, and you'll very likely lose their confidence and trust.

Here are five benefits you can gain by fully accepting your responsibilities:

1. **You'll learn to take the initiative**. You won't wait for your company or your boss to tell you what you ought to do. You'll be doing it while they're still thinking about it. You'll have the solution before they've even discovered the problem.

2. **You'll increase your professional stature**. When you look for additional responsibilities, and when you are willing to accept complete responsibility for your own actions, you'll develop yourself professionally and increase your management and executive abilities.

3. **You'll gain the respect and confidence of your superiors**. Employers always respect a person who has the courage to take a calculated risk, make a sound decision, and then accept full responsibility for his actions. They know that if you won't take a chance—if you won't stick your neck out once in a while—you don't have what it takes for a top-management job.

4. **You'll gain the loyalty, cooperation, and support of your subordinates**. When your subordinates realize that you'll assume responsibility not only for your own actions *but also for theirs,* you'll gain their full cooperation, and their loyal support. They'll do exactly what you ask them to do.

5. **When you look for responsibility, it will always find you**. Whenever leaders look for responsibility, somehow it always finds them. You cannot become a successful manager or a top executive in your chosen field unless you really do look for bigger and higher responsibilities. Waiting for responsibility to come your way is never enough. You must go out and find it.

Here is how you can accept full responsibility for your actions:

✔ *You must be decisive.* Be willing to assume the responsibility for your assessment of the facts and your estimate of the situation in any given set of circumstances. Do that and you'll motivate your subordinates to be confident and decisive and to accept their own responsibilities, too.

✔ *When you goof, admit it.* When you make a mistake, don't try to rationalize away your errors, look for a scapegoat, or go off and sit in a corner and sulk. Neither your superiors nor your subordinates expect you to be infallible, so you won't lose face when you admit you're wrong. When you do make a mistake and admit it, everyone will gain confidence in your honesty, an asset that is beyond price to any manager or executive.

✔ *Accept correction gracefully.* This can be hard to do if you have a thin skin. If correction bothers you, ask yourself these three questions:
  • Who is correcting me?
  • What are his or her qualifications to correct me?
  • Why is he or she correcting me?

Questions like these will help you judge the validity of your critic's comments and the motives behind them. After you've heard the person out, weigh his or her remarks carefully. Were they really true? Did you have it coming to you? Did the person have all the facts, or was he or she generalizing? If what was said makes sense, then accept the correction willingly and gracefully, correct the mistakes that have been brought to your attention, and thank the person for his or her help.

✔ *Accept the responsibility for the failures of your subordinates.* What it really comes down to here is determining what your own responsibility is first of all. If you're being paid to see that the job is done, then you'll have to assume the responsibility for the failure of your subordinates if it isn't.

Now I'll admit that it's easy to take the credit—but tough to take the blame—when you make a mistake. And when your boss corrects you not only for your failures but also for the failures of those who work for you, that's doubly hard to swallow. But that's one of the occupational hazards of being a manager. It goes with the territory.

✔ **You are also responsible for what you fail to do.** One of the common mistakes young managers and executives (and a lot of old ones, too) make is not to realize that they're also as responsible for what they *didn't do* as they are for what they *did do.*

In other words, the mistakes of *omission* will often outweigh the mistakes of *commission.* Assumption of individual responsibility covers not only what you do, but also what you fail to do. As an old preacher friend of mine puts it: "Just being good will never get you into heaven; you've got to be good for something."

✔ **Ask for a more responsible assignment.** W. R. Nelson, a top executive with one of the major automobile manufacturers, told me this: "We expect our young executives to be highly vocal—to speak up if they want more responsibility. They should go to their bosses and ask for it—and, if necessary, they should fight for it.

"We do all we can to encourage people to reach out for wider experience and more authority. But we can't read their minds. When a junior executive asks for more responsibility, we know that he wants it, and if we feel he's ready for it, he'll get it. If he can handle it, fine. If he can't, the sooner he finds out, the better for both of us."

Last, let me say, know every facet of your superior's job. Learn his duties completely and thoroughly. Be prepared to take over his job and his responsibilities, either temporarily or permanently, at a moment's notice. That is one of the best ways I know of to be ready to accept more responsibility.

SOLUTIONS: HOW TO GET YOUR STAFF TO ACCEPT RESPONSIBILITY

"An employee who'll do his best work only when the boss is around isn't worth having," says Harrison Rhyan, manager of a large electronics plant in Atlanta, Georgia. "We can't use people like that. Why, just look at the size of this place. We have three shifts and more than three thousand employees turning out television sets, radios, computers, and other electronic components of all kinds twenty-four hours a day. I can't live there around the clock, so unless your employees have a feeling of deep responsibility to the company to do their best, we couldn't manage to turn out the fine quality products that we do.

"I've tried a lot of methods throughout my years here to develop a strong sense of responsibility in my employees. The one I personally have found to be the most effective is to give the person the authority to make his or her own decisions. I'll go even further than that. I'll say that you will never be able to develop a complete sense of responsibility in a person until you force him or her to make their own decisions.

"Unless you do that, you'll find you're doing the job the production superintendent and the foremen ought to be doing. And they'll be making the decisions that belong to their supervisors. And the supervisors will actually be doing work on the assembly line that you're paying capable and qualified production employees to do.

"I'm not saying that you can abdicate your own responsibility, but a one-person act is evidence of poor management. A good manager will patiently and carefully instruct his subordinates to make sure they know what is expected of them. He can have them present their plans for doing the work to him for approval. But once approved, he will insist that they get their jobs done without minute guidance and detailed supervision.

"When you give your employees full responsibility to do their own work, when you give them the authority to make their own decisions, when you underwrite their mistakes, you'll encourage and motivate them to exercise initiative and to accept full responsibility for doing the job properly. You'll help them develop into more effective individuals and more reliable employees. In the end, you'll have a much more efficient organization than if you were to keep the responsibility and authority all to yourself."

The best way you can do what Harrison Rhyan said to do is to *use mission-type orders.* What is a mission-type order? *A mission-type order tells a person what you want done, but it doesn't tell him or her how to do it.* The *how* to is left entirely up to the individual carrying out your order.

A mission-type order says what your desired results are, but it doesn't tell your subordinate the methods to be used to achieve those results. It emphasizes skill, not rules.

When you use this kind of an order, you open the door wide for your employees to use their initiative, their imagination, and their ingenuity to solve the problems you've given to them.

If you've never used mission-type orders before, you're going to be pleasantly surprised when you do, for they'll give your organization a flexibility you never thought possible.

This will be especially apparent if you've been used to running a one-person show and not letting your subordinates carry out the details of the work. You'll suddenly find you have better employees than you thought you had.

About the only time you'll need to step in is when an overly zealous subordinate risks the health or safety of his people in getting the job done. If that happens, you'll have to exert your authority as the manager and take over temporarily. As soon as things are back under control and your subordinate understands the mistake, give him the responsibility again. If he can't handle it after that, you may have to let him go.

When you give responsibility, give authority, too.

You can't delegate the responsibility for getting the job done if you don't at the same time give the person the authority to carry out those responsibilities. Whenever you give a person the responsibility to do a specific job, you must also give him the authority to do it. *Authority and responsibility go hand in hand.* You cannot separate them.

"The delegation of authority commensurate with the responsibility develops a mutual confidence and respect between you and your subordinates," says Elaine Higgins, the manager of a New Jersey women's clothing manufacturing firm. "It also encourages your subordinates to exercise their initiative to get the job done, and at the same time, to give you their whole-hearted cooperation."

You can use the J. C. Penney method.

The J. C. Penney Company is well known for giving people the authority to carry out their responsibilities. In the Penney system the store manager is the key person. She is held completely responsible for the management and operation of her own store. At the same time, she is given the full authority to run that store.

She hires and trains her employees: the salespeople and clerks. She makes the decisions about her own local advertising. She orders most of her stock from lists and samples sent to her by the Penney headquarters, but she chooses what she wants. She is not required to accept any items that she feels are not suitable for her own locality.

In short, she runs her store on a completely decentralized basis, as if it were her very own, with nothing more than gentle policy guidance from the top. Her only requirement is to run the store at a reasonable profit.

As an executive and a manager, you too will demonstrate faith in your subordinates when you give them the authority to do the job along with the responsibility for doing it. Do that and you'll increase their desire to accept more and greater responsibility.

Hold your subordinate accountable for the results.

When we talk about responsibility and authority, there is one more word that we must consider: *accountability.*

For instance, your subordinates must know what their responsibilities are—what authority they have—and they must also understand that they will be held accountable for their actions. Unless this last part is fully understood, you won't be able to get the results you want.

"All employees in our company must be ready to account for the results of their daily work," says Fred L. Owens, the director of quality control for a manufacturer of fine mobile homes, travel trailers, and motor homes in Indiana. "If the results are not favorable and not properly accounted for, then corrective action must be taken.

"It is imperative, though, that before you give anyone responsibility, he must know that his authority is to carry out that responsibility. Only then can you properly hold the person strictly accountable for the results.

"This principle applies to all areas in our company. If any single superior is reluctant to hold one of his people accountable for results, then he or she must be ready to explain, and if necessary, to accept the consequences for their failures. This is a requirement of ours at all levels of management and supervision, from the top to the bottom. There are no exceptions."

In conclusion, let me say that your subordinates must have a clear understanding of what is expected of them. They must know what their responsibilities are and what authority they have. Then you must hold them strictly accountable for their actions. If mistakes are made, correct them without hesitation. When you do that, you'll get the results that you want and expect. You'll have developed a sense of responsibility in your subordinates.

SOLUTIONS: HOW TO MAKE SURE YOUR SUBORDINATES KNOW WHAT YOU WANT DONE

Your subordinates will do their best for you when they know exactly what their jobs are. Many times a person fails to do a proper job because he didn't understand what you wanted done in the first place.

Ambiguity, indecisiveness, vagueness, and incompleteness of orders are more often to blame for failure to comply with your orders than is disobedience. It's up to you to tell your employees specifically what you expect from them, when and where you want it, and then to supervise to make sure you get what you want. Do this and you'll get results; people will do the best they can.

The first thing you must do is to issue positive orders that are easy to understand. The best way to do that is to *use simple words and simple terms.* I have actually seen people go out of their way to use big words to drive another person to the dictionary. Then they wondered why their orders were not obeyed.

Perhaps they wanted to appear wise and well-educated. If that was their objective, they defeated their purpose. I once knew an army officer who loved to use such words as *obfuscate,* for instance. If confusion was his goal, he most certainly succeeded, for the word *obfuscate* means to *cloud, confuse, darken,* or *muddle.*

Instead of using such simple verbs as *make* or *do,* Captain J. L. used *construct, fabricate, accomplish, consummate,* or *effect.* He never *started* anything; instead, he *initiated, commenced,* or *inaugurated* everything. He never *sent* a message; he always *trans-*

mitted, *communicated,* or *forwarded* it. Nor did he send out information; he *circulated* it or *promulgated* it or *disseminated* it.

Never did he use such little words as *if, so, for,* and *but.* He always made sure to replace them with such clumsy phrases as *in the event that, therefore, on behalf of, nevertheless.* Captain J. L. might have admitted on occasion that some of the "governmental federalese" needed improvement, but he always wanted you to say *amelioration!*

Let me wrap up this idea of using simple words and phrases by advising you to stick to two- and three-syllable words whenever possible. It's the simplest things that last longest and wear best. The simplest writing is the best writing because it's the easiest to understand. Speaking of simple writing and using two- and three-syllable words reminds me of a letter I once received from a California reader of one of my books. Her letter said, "Thank you for writing a book that I was able to understand on the first reading."

Nearly two thousand years ago a man who walked by the Sea of Galilee understood the principle of simplicity well. Everything in His life was simple: His clothing and His food; His stories and His parables; His language and His words. Yet His message is still studied today, for even though complicated by men, the order He gave was clear, concise, positive, and easy to understand when He said simply, *"Follow me."*

Know what you want before you issue an order.

It's important to know exactly what you want to get done before you tell anyone to do anything. Too many orders grow like a rambling rose, creeping ivy, or the crab grass in my lawn. If you aren't sure of the results you want, then you're not yet ready to issue an order.

To help you determine the results you want first, follow these simple guidelines each time so you can establish the right thinking pattern:

✔ *What* exactly is it that I want to get done?

✔ *Who* is going to do this job for me?

✔ *When* does the job have to be done?

✔ *Why* does it have to be done?

✔ *Where* is the best place to do the job?

✔ *How* will it be done?

If you box yourself into a corner by forcing yourself to answer such relevant questions as *what, who, when, why, where,* and *how,* you can't help but improve your abilities to make sure the job is understood and accomplished.

You can check to see if your orders are understood by using three techniques:

1. Have people repeat oral orders to you.

2. Have them ask you questions if they don't understand.

3. Ask people questions to see if they understand your order.

Let's discuss each of those techniques, starting with

1. **Have oral orders repeated to you**. "Following this simple rule does two things for you," says Stanley Adams, a variety store owner in Orlando, Florida. "First of all, you know for sure whether or not your listener understood your instructions. Second, it gives you a chance to check on yourself so you'll know if you actually said what you wanted to say."

I can think of no exception to this rule. If people misinterpret your orders or your instructions, it's a cinch you won't get the results you want.

So make this a hard-and-fast rule to follow. Paste it in your hat. Oh, I know that once in a while people will get irritated and think you're insulting their intelligence when you ask them to repeat your order. Well, they'll just have to feel that way. Don't worry; they'll get over it.

2. **Have them ask you questions if they don't understand**. Normally, if a person doesn't understand exactly what you want done, he'll ask you to clarify it. You can help the process along by asking, "Are there any questions?"

If you're giving instructions to a group, don't assume everything's completely understood just because no one asks a question. Many times a person will have a question, or there'll be a point she doesn't understand, but she doesn't want to appear ignorant in front of the group.

Remember your high school days. The teacher asks, "Are there any questions?" Not a hand goes up. "Class is dismissed, then," the teacher says, and immediately half a dozen students who were afraid they'd appear stupid in front of the others flock around the desk to have some point explained.

3. ***Ask them questions to see if they understand your order.*** If your subordinates don't ask you questions, you should ask them questions yourself. Let me preface this point by saying that whenever you issue oral orders that have more than three major points to remember, have your listeners take notes.

Then you can ask questions like this without hurting anyone's feelings: "Annie, would you look at your notes there—did I say two or three?" You know what you said. You just want to be sure that Annie and everybody else knows.

Always use your established chain of authority to issue your orders.

No matter how big or how small your organization is, it will always have a definite fixed line of authority through which orders, commands, or instructions are given.

It's absolutely essential that you use this line of authority when you issue instructions. To bypass the foreman or the supervisor is not only a violation of good management procedure, it can also be confusing to the employee if the order you issue conflicts with the one received previously from the immediate supervisor.

The last step in issuing orders that will be carried out is supervision. That subject is too big to cover here, so I'll discuss it in detail on the following pages.

SOLUTIONS: INSPECT YOUR SUBORDINATES' WORK

Now that I've discussed how to make sure the job was properly understood to be accomplished, let's discuss the subject of supervision.

"One of the most neglected areas in management is inspecting the operation," says Walter T. Erwin, vice-president in charge of all production for a large midwestern manufacturing corporation. "Yet it's one of the most important aspects of your work if you really want to make sure the job gets done properly.

"A manager can think up a lot of excuses to keep from leaving his desk and getting out into the actual production area. For one thing, he too often construes his primary duties to be paper work. If he goes on an inspection tour, his in-box seems to overflow with correspondence that should've been answered yesterday when he gets back.

"Then he'll always have a stack of telephone messages that piled up during his absence, and these have to be taken care of, too. But correspondence and phone calls aren't really the main part of a manager's job. They are merely by-products of his real job—they are the red tape that goes along with it.

"Of course there are several more reasons why a manager hates to get out from behind his desk to inspect the operation. For one thing, many managers simply don't have the technical knowledge they need to conduct an inspection properly. They don't know the actual details of their own operation well enough to really tell when something is wrong, and they're afraid of looking like a fool out in front of their own employees. No wonder they don't want to leave their office. It's a lot safer in there!"

Now what Mr. Erwin says is true, and I know that executives and managers work primarily with people while technicians work with things. However, these problems can be solved. To become a good inspector, you must know your business inside out. This takes study, planning, and practice. With constant study, you will know before you inspect what is correct and what is not correct in your particular area of responsibility.

Planning is required so that you can schedule your inspections in such a way that over a period of time you'll be able to inspect all aspects of your operation. With practice you'll be able to tell at once what is being done right and what is being done wrong. Yes, it does take a lot of work to conduct a personal inspection properly, but that is your duty as a manager, for *an organization usually does a good job only when the boss inspects the work.* There's another old phrase that will pay you dividends to keep in mind, and that is *never inspected . . . always neglected!* So here is

A Fail-Safe Seven-Step Inspection Procedure

1. *Set aside a specific amount of time for your inspections.* Inspect some phase of your operation every single working day. But don't inspect the same thing at the same time every day. Change things around. Sometimes inspect in the morning, sometimes in the afternoon. If you have a two- or three-shift operation, do some of your inspecting at night. Don't let anyone get off inspection-free!

Monday mornings and Friday afternoons are the most critical periods of the week. Or at least the first four hours and the last four hours of your work week are, whatever your schedule. These are the start-up and let-down periods, when your employees are more careless and do their worst work. So bear down on your inspections at those times more than at any other. The first day of deer hunting or trout fishing may also fall into that category.

2. *Go over your inspection points before you inspect.* Study and review your selected points of inspection before you inspect. That way you won't get caught short; your employees won't be able to make a fool of you. You'll always appear to be an expert, and, in fact, before long you will be. I recommend that you select no less than three and no more than eight points to inspect at any one time. By changing these points every day, you'll soon be able to cover your entire operation.

3. *Inspect only your selected points.* Carefully go over your selected inspection points before you make your inspection. And then when you inspect, *don't look at anything else. Don't try to be the expert on everything in one single day.* You can't do it. Stick to your system and don't let anyone distract you. You'll cover everything in good time.

4. *When you inspect, emphasize.* Emphasize the points you have selected for your inspection, *not the points your subordinate is trying to emphasize for you.* This can become a cat-and-mouse game if you let it get away from you. Just remember who's inspecting and who's being inspected.

The moment you let your subordinate lead you away from your selected inspection points, you'll no longer be the expert. Then you'll be running the risk of exposing your lack of knowledge on the subject your subordinate has picked.

You must retain control of the situation so you can always appear to be the expert. Time, experience, study, and practice will make you one.

5. *Bypass the chain of authority.* This is an absolute must— no exceptions. No other kind of inspection is ever satisfactory. Don't ask your subordinate managers how they're getting along and how things are going. You know the answer you'll get. You must get down to the actual working level so you can see for yourself what's really happening.

Of course, as a matter of courtesy, the manager of that particular section or department should go with you on your inspection tour, but don't ask her the questions you want answered—ask the people who work for her. That's the only way you'll ever get the straight answers you need.

6. *When you inspect, listen.* Don't talk except to ask questions. To keep from getting mousetrapped during an inspection, never ask a question to which you don't already know the answer. Remember that you're inspecting to see if your subordinates also know the correct answers.

7. *Recheck the mistakes you find.* An inspection is of no value unless you take the necessary action to correct the mistakes you find. So follow up. Reinspect. Supervise and make sure your corrective orders are being carried out. Remember that an order without supervision is usually the same as no order at all.

SOLUTIONS: HOW TO BE A TOUGH INSPECTOR YET STILL BE LIKED

I realize that as a manager your job is to manage and supervise people, not to win a popularity contest. But it's still a lot better if you can do your job and be liked and respected at the same time. Here are six brief guidelines you can use to attain that goal when conducting your daily inspections:

1. *Don't take sides with labor against your superiors.* During your inspections, don't criticize your boss in any way. This is a cheap way to try to win popularity with subordinates, and it doesn't work in the long run. Those employees will lose respect not only for your boss but also for you. You'll only defeat your purpose and lose your credibility at the same time.

2. *Praise the supervisor or local section manager* whose subordinates you're inspecting—even if you find problems or mistakes in their operation. Always support the "boss" in front of her people. Never criticize her in front of them. Do that, and they'll lose all their respect for her. They'll never trust her judgment or have confidence in her again. If she needs to be replaced, then do so, but if you're going to keep her in her management slot, then back her to the hilt.

3. *Correct his mistakes in private.* If things aren't what they should be, take him aside to counsel him. Even then, make sure you *correct only the mistakes. Don't criticize the person for making them.* And when you do correct his errors, praise him first. It'll take a lot of the sting out of your correction.

4. *Don't generalize—be specific.* Tell her exactly and precisely what is wrong. Don't take it out on her for something someone else has done. And, don't try to punish everyone for the mistakes of only one individual. Pin the tail on the right donkey.

5. *Let the supervisor or local section manager explain his side.* Don't correct him until you understand why he's doing it that way. It could be that he has a perfectly logical explanation for doing things that way. Many times local conditions cause the development of certain odd procedures. So find out first before you jump. Give him a chance to explain it to you.

6. *Don't harass—just inspect.* Need I say more?

Here I've given you six guidelines you can use to become adept at making inspections. I'm sure you can come up with some ideas of your own to supplement them. But whatever you do, please keep this one thought clearly in mind:

Never Inspected—Always Neglected!

SOLUTIONS: HOW TO GET YOUR SUBORDINATES TO GIVE MAXIMUM EFFORT

If you want to get the best out of your subordinates, set a high standard of performance for your organization. What you do, what you say, and how you yourself act will have a major bearing on whether you're able to get the maximum effort from your subordinates. If you give only the minimum yourself, you have no right to expect the maximum from them.

For instance, if you straggle into work late and leave early, if you're careless about the quality of their work, if you're not interested in the amount of production or its quality, if you act bored with your own job, then your subordinates will no doubt assume the same attitude about their work, too.

But if you set the right example by always giving the maximum yourself, others will do the same. Enthusiasm is contagious. If you're positive, enthusiastic, and excited about your work, chances are great that your subordinates will feel that way, too.

"I've never met a successful manager of people who was not highly motivated too," says William A. Doane, the safety director of an Oklahoma petroleum company. "The best motivators are those people who are themselves hard workers to the point of maximum commitment to their jobs.

"Managers like these motivate their employees largely by example. And employees like to feel they're living up to the high standards the boss sets, especially when the boss is giving the maximum to the job of making the department or company highly successful."

Don't accept the present system as the best or only way if you want to go for the maximum.

A lot of people are the victims of *status-quo thinking.* Just because they've always done a certain job a certain way, they assume it's the best possible method, perhaps the only one. So they resist change. They find the idea that they must alter their behavior or their thought patterns in some way not only uncomfortable but sometimes even frightening.

Almost any activity, however, can be improved with just a little thought and some extra effort. Change is indispensable to progress, and progress comes only with change.

Change always starts with an idea. Here are some methods that Christina Ireland, the director of a chemical company's special projects division, says you can use to change the status quo and revamp your present system so you can go for the maximum:

"Reexamine your thinking.

Repress old ideas and solutions; push the accepted methods aside temporarily while you look for new methods. Examine new ideas with the uninhibited curiosity of a child. Develop the knack of seeing things as if you were looking at them for the very first time.

"Do some brainstorming with other people.

Probe the minds of others. Use questions to stimulate thinking. The method here is to suspend critical judgment while suggesting new ideas. There's plenty of time for evaluation later. Now you want as many new ideas as possible. So no matter how crazy an idea sounds, jot it down. You must create a freewheeling atmosphere to get the most out of brainstorming.

"Keep your imagination turned on all the time.

Don't turn your brain off when you go home from work. Fresh ideas can pop up all the time—during a conversation with a friend, while reading a newspaper or magazine, walking, showering, putting on your makeup, shaving, eating. You can force your mind to work all the time if you will. Keep a notebook handy. You never know when that idea is going to come, and you don't want to miss it.

"Be willing to accept new ideas.

It's easy to come up with all sorts of reasons why something new won't work. If you want your people to do their best to come up with new ideas and ways of doing things, then you must keep an open mind. You must be willing to give their ideas a fair try.

Whenever you arbitrarily push a new idea to the side, you're hammering another nail into the coffin of a dying organization. You can't get the maximum out of your subordinates that way. Any company that refuses to accept new methods or even to listen to new ideas is not growing. It's not even standing still. In fact, it's not only going backward—it's dying!

How you can help people set goals for themselves.

If you want to get people to give their maximum for you, you must teach them how to set personal goals for themselves. A lot of people just seem to drift along in a never-never land. They have some vague, indefinite ideas about what they want out of life, but they never seem to be able to come up with any concrete, specific plans on how to get it.

One of the best ways I know of to get the maximum efforts out of people is to *help them determine what they want most out of life and then show them how to get it.* To make an individual goal-minded on the job to give the maximum, use these six techniques.

1. **Make his goal specific.** To get your subordinate out of that vague dream world, make him get specific about what he wants from you. For instance, is he aiming for more money—for financial security? Is he interested in a better job or promotion? Does he have his sights set on a certain position in the company? Then do anything and everything you can to help him make his goal specific and concrete.

2. **Help her develop a plan for achieving her goal.** Show her what she has to do to attain her goal. If more education or training is required, tell her exactly what will be needed. Have her get her own goal down in writing; that will help her know whether or not she really wants to put out that extra effort.

3. **Make his goal exciting and worthwhile.** Help him see how he'll benefit when he reaches his goal. Kindle his desire for success by enumerating the material rewards and psychic benefits that will be his. Remember that *desire is the first law of gain.* A person must want to succeed before he ever will.

4. **Let her compete with herself.** When a person fails to beat her own record, she can take it a lot better than when she's defeated by someone else. Her target can be a quota or a record she wants

to break, a standard she wants to improve, a new completion time she wants to establish—any impersonal target other than competition with another human being.

5. *Make his goal attainable.* Be sure that his goal is realistic, reasonable, and attainable. To have a man with an eighth-grade education make his goal a position that requires a Ph.D. in chemistry would be foolish. Yet people often give themselves an impossible goal and then give up completely on everything else when they don't attain it.

6. *Reward her when she succeeds.* Don't promise her a reward unless you can fulfill your promises when she does succeed. As Elmer Wheeler, one of America's top salespeople, used to say, "Don't sell a person an empty box."

To get a person to give the maximum, instill a feeling of pride in the job.

No matter what the job is, every person wants to take pride in what he or she does. The desire for praise, attention, and approval is one of the most powerful incentives to which every single person will respond.

Unless a person is proud of himself, his job, and his organization, you cannot possibly get the maximum from him. It just can't be done.

There are still other techniques you can use to go for the maximum instead of just placidly accepting the minimum. For instance, you can throw down a challenge; you can give people a cause to fight for; you can set up tests for maximum potential by giving a person a bigger job to do; you can give people the chance to tell you how they need to improve. I'm sure you can think of many, many more.

Watch for these tell-tale signs of minimum performance.

To wrap up, I want you to know how to detect the signs and symptoms of minimum performance by management in your organization.

1. Management is no longer willing to experiment, to take chances, or to try new methods and new ideas.

2. The company is no longer looking for new markets and new customers but is satisfied to hold on to what it has.

3. The organization demands absolute conformity from its employees. It attracts only passive, dependent people to its work force.

4. Promotion is based only on seniority, not on performance.

5. Management is self-satisfied. It no longer has a program of self-development and self-improvement.

6. The organization is a boring place to work. It is dull, lifeless, and presents no challenges to its employees.

SOLUTIONS: HOW TO CONTROL YOUR EMOTIONS ON THE JOB

As a manager or an executive, you need to have your employees trust you and feel that your behavior is predictable. Of course, everyone blows up from time to time. Every one of us has a breaking point where just one more little thing will make us blow our stacks.

If you can be consistent in your actions and your conduct, however, people will trust and respect you. If you are not, chances are you won't last long as an executive or a manager, for executives must work with people.

For example, if you're subject to uncontrollable outbursts of anger, you'll have difficulty gaining and holding the respect of your employees. They'll never know for sure what your reactions are going to be when they bring problems to you. As their superior, you must be consistent.

If you can't control yourself, you can't control others.

If you do happen to have a tendency to be easily irritated by small things, if by nature you seem to have been given a sour disposition, if you display frequent temper tantrums as a spoiled child would, then you must get rid of those bad habits.

It isn't just a matter of getting people to like you, although that's important, too. If you're in a leadership position, it's really a matter of getting them to work for you, to do what you ask them to do, to inspire them to put out their best efforts.

If you let your bad temper and sour disposition creep in, this will show your subordinates that you lack self-discipline and self-control. They'll know you can never be depended on to do the right thing in an emergency.

A fit of anger usually indicates that you don't have complete confidence in yourself and in your own abilities. You're probably running scared of your boss or afraid of losing your job. At any rate, you'd best remember that if you can't control yourself, you can never begin to control others.

Determine your anger and frustration triggers. Identify for yourself what turns you into a raging maniac. Being aware of what upsets you can help you adopt a more responsible reaction. Here is a list of anger triggers that get to most people on the job.

1. Having people put you down or make you look stupid in front of others.

2. Listening to endless chit-chat about subjects not related to the business.

3. Putting up with constant tardiness or absenteeism.

4. Seeing discourteous treatment of your secretary or your assistant.

5. Being lied to.

6. Having a confidence betrayed.

7. Working with someone who refuses to admit mistakes.

8. Being constantly interrupted in meetings or in the middle of a conversation.

9. Having someone finish your sentence for you.

10. Having your boss or an associate constantly criticize the way you look or the way you dress.

11. Being stood up for an appointment.

12. Being unfairly criticized without being given the chance to respond or explain.

13. Seeing a co-worker or an associate constantly break established company rules and regulations.

Now here are some tips on how to master your anger completely so you can keep these things from upsetting you:

"A person is just as big as the things that make him mad," says Lewis Evans, a retired midwestern restaurant owner now living in Florida. "And in the restaurant business, a lot of things happen that could really get you down if you'd allow them to.

"I always tried to keep two things in mind when I was in business and dealing with people to make my living. One was this: *Never let someone else's inferiority overcome your superiority.* The second one was this: *When things go wrong or someone makes you real angry, instead of flying off into a great rage, fly off into a great calm.* It's a heck of a lot better for your disposition as well as for your stomach and your heart."

Kevin Duffy, the director of industrial relations for a large California company, told me: "I've learned a few things in my life of working with others, and one thing I have learned is this, *Never yell at a person unless he's so far away you have to shout to make him hear you.* And even then, make sure he understands why you're shouting or yelling at him. Shouting or yelling at a person at any other time has no value whatever. It only creates trouble for you."

Above all, don't swear at people. Never let your emotions enter the picture when you're correcting someone's mistake. *Always correct the mistake, but never criticize the person for making it.* The moment you become angry in your attempt to correct another person's mistakes, the issue becomes cloudy and obscure. The result will be nothing more than a shouting match between two combatants.

Another good way to keep from getting angry yourself is to use humor to appease the other person's anger. My daughter-in-law is extremely short, only four feet nine inches tall. Her job is to fill requests from various department managers for supplies, so she is often the target of their bad dispositions.

Whenever one of them gets too abusive with her, she climbs up on a stool and says, "Well, at least now we can see eye to eye on this!" It never fails to crack up the angriest of managers and help him to get over his mad spell.

SOLUTIONS: HOW TO TREAT YOUR EMPLOYEES AS INDIVIDUALS

Industrial psychologists say that one of the biggest mistakes managers and executives can make is treating employees and subordinates like machines or equipment instead of treating them as individuals—real, live people.

Let's face it. Not one of the people who work under you wants to be a nobody. Every one of them wants to be somebody. No one wants to be just another number. *Everyone wants to retain his or her own special individual identity.*

All sorts of psychological studies have shown that morale and job performance of average workers is higher when the boss takes a personal interest in them and treats them as individuals.

Most managers will admit that it's vital to make their subordinates feel important, but they don't take time to do so. They're much too busy with more significant things, they say, so they go right on ignoring their employees. The end result? Employee morale nosedives; so does both the quantity and quality of production. Absenteeism goes up; so do employee grievances.

But it is not really that difficult to treat people as individuals. Besides, it doesn't take that much time. Fifteen or twenty minutes invested daily can save you countless hours of listening to formal labor grievances or sitting in nonproductive, unprofitable arbitration hearings. There are three simple techniques you can use to get to know your employees better and make them feel important as individuals at the same time:

1. *Know each person by his or her first name.* A person's name is the most important word in all the world to him or her. To use it can often work what seems like *white magic*. But if you don't call the person by name, if you don't even know his or her name, if you forget it or mispronounce it, this will work in reverse for you, like *black magic!*

As a good manager, you should be able to call every single one of your employees, not only by their last, but by their first names as well. It's one of the most powerful, most convincing ways you can say to a person: *I recognize you as an important individual.*

"Today I know *every* single person in the plant by his or her first name," says Roy Hayes, president of a Chicago musical instrument manufacturing company employing nearly 500 people.

"Oh, I miss once in a while, especially if the person is real new, but not very often. But it wasn't always that way. Used to be, I never paid any attention at all to my employees. I knew the main department heads and I figured that was enough.

"One day I saw a group of men standing around doing nothing. I went up to them, chewed them out for loafing on the job, and told them to get back to work. Said I hadn't hired them to stand around and if that was all they could find to do, I'd fire them.

"Well, they just laughed at me. So did all the people watching. That made it even worse. I became furious and blew my top! Made a complete fool out of myself in front of all my employees.

"I found out they didn't even work for me! You see, we lease the building and the landlord had sent over some electrical workers to repair the heating and cooling system. They were waiting for their own foreman to tell them what to do.

"Since then, I've made it a point to know *every* one of my people. I've kept everything on a personal first-name basis here. It's paid off for me in friendship, loyalty, cooperation, and quality production."

If you want the same kind of results for yourself, then treat your subordinates as people—not cattle. There's a lot of difference between a *team* and a *herd*. People want to be known by their names, not by their clock numbers, "Hey you!", or "Fellas." It doesn't cost you a penny more to call a person by his or her first name, but it makes them feel like a million bucks.

2. *Praise them—pat them on the back for their work.* As I said earlier, Charles Schwab was paid a million dollars a year by Andrew Carnegie because he knew the secret of how to get the best out of people. Mr. Schwab said in effect: "As far as I'm concerned, the only way to inspire a person to do his or her level best is by individual appreciation, praise, and encouragement."

Your employees will respond to praise, too. That's human nature. So remember, the second way to treat your subordinates as individuals and make them feel more important is to *praise and compliment them for what they do.*

Frankly, I have yet to meet the person who doesn't appreciate a compliment or a pat on the back for what he's done. A compliment can serve as a strong incentive, too. My wife's beauty operator, Carolyn Webb, says, "I can lose more weight with a compliment from my husband about how good I look than I ever can with my doctor's threat of a heart attack from being overweight!"

3. *"Show respect for a person's knowledge and skill,"* says Arlie Atwood, a general foreman with an Arizona copper company.

"For instance, just the other day I was watching one of our machine operators, Wally Brown. I marveled at the smoothness of his actions: the sure, deft, rhythmic way he handled his raw materials and his equipment. And I told him so. I said, 'Wally, you absolutely amaze me. Why, I'd never in the world be able to do that as well as you do.'

"Wally looked up at me from his bench and grinned. 'Well, I should hope not,' he said. 'If you could, I might find myself out of a job!'

"Now I sincerely meant what I said to Wally. I do have a deep respect for his abilities, his knowledge, and his skills. I wanted him to know that I do. But if I didn't tell him, he'd never know how I feel."

As Will Rogers used to say, "Everybody's ignorant, 'cept on different things." Chances are, every person you supervise knows more about his or her own individual operation than you do. And that's the way it should be.

So if you want to make your employees feel good, if you want them to feel important, then remember to use this third technique: *Show respect for the person's knowledge and skills.*

I know there is no magic formula that you can use to guarantee results, but I also know that when you treat every person as an important individual—when you make every single one of them important to you—the morale, efficiency, and productivity of your organization cannot help but go up, and that makes all your extra efforts worthwhile.

Succeeding in Your Own Business

If you're in your own business now, learn the best techniques you can use to advertise and let your business talk for you even when you're home and sound asleep in bed, on vacation, or out of town.

To succeed in your own business, you must let people know who you are, where you are, and what service or product you're offering. Here are nine ways you can do that:

1. *Have a big sign—a gigantic one!* Make your sign the biggest one in the whole town, one that can be seen and read twenty-four hours a day. People should be able to read it plainly in the daytime, and it should proclaim your name and your business in big neon letters after dark.

Let your sign work for you twenty-four hours a day. This is the most effective and inexpensive advertising you can use. As one highly successful businesswoman told me, "I want everyone to remember the name of my business, and advertising with a big outdoor sign is the best and least expensive way I can do that. After my initial cost of installation, the maintenance is negligible."

One of the best signs I've ever seen was a huge one of a Dutch girl with wooden shoes, a big broom, and a sunbonnet in a small town in Iowa. The sign above her head read SUPERMAID CAFE. It was simple in design, yet unforgettable.

2. *Use your windows as silent salespeople.* Your window displays can easily pay for 25 percent of your overhead if you use them as silent salespeople. Keep the lights on in your store windows and let them work for you twenty-four hours a day, just as your big outdoor sign does.

3. *Let your store shelves and counters sell for you, too.* Well-displayed articles are already half sold. Letting people wait on themselves and pick their purchases off the counters and the shelves is the key to success in big discount stores and supermarkets. Items behind the counter don't sell nearly so well as those in the aisles. If people can't see what you have to sell, then they won't buy it.

4. *Friendly and cheerful employees sell for you.* I drive nearly two miles to a supermarket because the one only two blocks from me has such surly, discourteous clerks. A cheerful, friendly face attracts customers. A sour face drives people away. A smile is one of the biggest assets your employees can have, so make sure they always wear one.

Tell them to leave their personal problems at home. Bill Thomas, a business friend of mine, told me that he was once complimented by one of his employees for coming to work every day with a big smile on his face and for never bringing his personal problems to the office with him.

"What he didn't know was that some mornings I had to stand outside the door and screw that smile on my face before I went into the office, but evidently it was worth my doing it," Bill said with a big laugh.

5. *Tie an easily remembered slogan to your business.* Give people something specific to remember you by. For example, a successful furniture store in a small Iowa farm town has a huge sign that says, "Brin's Furniture Store Around the Corner on Seneca." That certainly is not an earthshaking slogan by any means, but it is unique enough for people to remember, for they come from miles around to buy their furniture at Brin's rather than go somewhere else.

6. *Use color to promote sales.* Bright colors are cheerful and attract customers. Paint your front door a brilliant red and let people know you're there. For instance, if you have a paint-and-wallpaper store, color is what you're selling above all else. Use color on your trucks, in your store, on your stationery, and on your wrapping paper. That's a natural for you to do.

7. *Advertise, advertise, advertise.* Advertise, even if it's only a few lines in the newspaper, on a billboard, or direct mail promotion. Doing business without advertising is like winking at a girl in the dark. *You* may know what you're doing, but no one else does. Maybe that sounds old fashioned to you, but it's still true.

You must do something to reach the person out there who gets to town only once in a while, and believe it or not, there are still a lot of people like that, especially in the Midwest in farm country.

You need to let those people know that you have shoes and suits or dresses and blouses or paint and brushes or whatever it is you're selling in your store. If you don't let them know, then some company or store down the street will tell them, and that store will end up with the business that could've been yours. Every potential customer is important to you, so go after all of them.

8. *When something new comes out, get it for your customers.* *New* is the greatest word in all merchandising. People always want the very latest thing, so give it to them. The two most used words in television advertising are *new* and *improved,* but they must work, for advertisers use them over and over again.

9. *Get all the free publicity you can.* If you can do it, get your company's name or your store's name in your local newspaper without using advertising to do so. A great many people, especially in a small town, are interested in news of local importance, for they can see all the latest world news on television. If you live in a big city with a large daily newspaper, this technique probably won't work for you. But in a small town where the paper is a small daily or weekly, it is usually starved for news and will gladly publish your item.

So if you can, get the name of your business in the newspaper when you have a wedding or an anniversary in your store or in your company. Tell the reporters about it. Have a photographer take pictures. This will give you free space in the news column where people can see your name. Publicity like that can't be bought for any price. What could be cheaper than that?

SOLUTIONS: TWENTY-FOUR TIPS ON HOW TO SUCCEED IN YOUR OWN BUSINESS

The fear of failure is the greatest fear a businessperson can have, so I want to give you twenty-four tips on how to succeed in your own business so you can avoid that fear.

Perhaps, even more than money, pride is on the line with a new business venture. The threat of failure will almost drive a person to do the unthinkable to make the business a resounding success.

A young couple going into the restaurant business told me this: "We simply have to succeed in this venture. Everything we have is in it, our savings, our home, the whole works. We just can't go down the drain. Death would be only slightly worse than our failure!"

To help them gain confidence, I told them this: "Never let the fear of failure enter your mind. If you think for one moment that you are going to fail, then you surely will, for *as you think, so shall you become*. But if you think that you will succeed, then you most certainly will, for you will be thinking positive thoughts of success, and the same concept is true, *you will become what you think about*."

Our conversation took place two years ago. Did it help them? I think it did. Their business is booming today in spite of competition from a cafeteria, a Chinese restaurant, a bagel shop, and a McDonald's all in the same shopping center.

That young couple had refused to think negative thoughts. Thinking positive thoughts helped them come up with new, creative ideas. They were able to use those ideas to make their restaurant more attractive and to create new, delicious items for their menu.

And now for those twenty-four tips for your business success:

1. Just as I told that young couple, never let the fear of failure enter your mind. Think only that you will be successful, for *as you think, so shall you become*.

2. Recognize what you can do best and use this talent to build your business. It is one of your greatest advantages, and no one can ever take the ability away from you.

3. Always promote the strengths of your business. Remember that your competitors are selling their strengths, too.

4. Compete by saying how good your products or your services are. Don't try to compete by badmouthing your competitors. Tactics like that will backfire and hurt you in the long run.

5. Remember that your customer's welfare, not yours, is always his primary concern. He wants to know exactly what you can do for him, not what he can do for you, and not what you've done for somebody else.

6. Treat your small accounts with respect, understanding, concern, and the expectation that some day they'll be big ones for you.

7. Don't assume that your prospects are ignorant if they don't understand your sales pitch the first time around—or even the second or third time that you give it. Could be that it's your sales pitch that's off base rather than their understanding.

8. Always think in terms of your customers' needs and then determine how you can best fill those needs for them.

9. Don't become too dependent on your "good" accounts for your business. Tomorrow they could be persuaded to take their business somewhere else. (Of course, you should keep on your toes to keep that from happening.)

10. Don't let temporary successes cause you to lower your standards, forget your ultimate goals, or let up, even a little.

11. Don't assume that everyone is as honest as you are, but don't think that everyone else is dishonest either.

12. Selling good-quality merchandise is your best bet if you want to succeed in business. Cheap-quality merchandise will not win you lasting customers. An old saying goes like this: Buying cheap to save money is like stopping a clock to save time. Neither one will work.

13. Two strong statements you can use to sell your products or your services are these: I can save you money, and I can help you make more money.

14. Don't try shoddy scheming or false claims to sell the customer. You may make the sale this time, but you'll drive off the customer in the long run. "Once burned, twice shy" will be the end result.

15. Keep up with what your customers want and need. Business is never static. Change is constant, so stay up to date. If some item isn't moving, get rid of it. Don't keep it in your inventory. Free that money for better uses.

16. Remember that someone will always have a lower price than you do. That means you must have better quality to justify your higher price.

17. You can never stop learning. You can never have too much information about your business. Organize your know-how and use it when and where it is needed to become more successful.

18. Build a reputation for honesty and integrity. It will win you customers who will stick with you.

19. There are no shortcuts to business success—those all lead down blind alleys. It takes plain, old-fashioned hard work to succeed in business, but if you want it enough, you can do it.

20. Always give your customer more for his money than your competitor does, either in quantity or in quality.

21. Give customers more than they pay for and make sure they know that when you do. If you sell him a suit, give him a matching handkerchief or a pair of socks to go with it as a special gift. If you sell her an expensive dress, a tiny vial of cologne as a small gift will help bring her back again.

22. Treat everyone you contact in your business with the same dignity and respect that you expect for yourself. This includes your customers, your co-workers, your employees—yes, and even your competitors, too.

23. Realize that you can't sell everyone everything, so don't be disheartened when you don't.

24. Cleanliness and appearance are remembered by the customer. If your company or store has public restrooms, be sure that they are always sparkling clean, for a dirty restroom will lose you customers.

SOLUTIONS: HOW YOUR ATTITUDE CAN INFLUENCE YOUR SUCCESS OR FAILURE

Your success or failure depends on how you think, for *you become what you think about*. If you think you will fail, you surely will, but if you think you will succeed, then you will succeed, for it all depends upon your attitude.

Let me tell you the story about the man who sold hot dogs:

There was a man who lived by the side of the road and sold hot dogs.

He was hard of hearing so he had no radio.

He had trouble with his eyes so he read no newspapers.

But he sold good hot dogs.

He put up signs on the highway telling how good they were.

He stood on the side of the road and cried: "Buy a hot dog, Mister?"

And people bought.

He increased his meat and bun orders.

He bought a bigger stove to take care of his trade.

He finally got his son home from college to help him out.

But then something happened.

His son said, "Father, haven't you been listening to the radio?

"Haven't you been reading the newspapers?

"There's a big depression.

"The European situation is terrible.

"The domestic situation is even worse."

Whereupon the father thought, "Well, my son's been to college, he reads the newspapers, and he listens to the radio, so he ought to know."

So the father cut down on his meat and bun orders, took down his advertising signs, and no longer bothered to stand out on the highway to sell his hot dogs.

And his hot dog sales fell almost overnight.

"You're right, son," the father said to the boy. "We certainly are in the middle of a great depression."

And so the man's business failed because of his changed attitude, for *he became what he thought about*. He was doing fine selling good hot dogs by the side of the road. Then he started thinking that things were falling apart, and they did, because of his attitude.

So if you want to succeed instead of fail, you must think about how you can be successful instead of worrying about being a failure. Here's a simple concept you can use to do that. The rule to success is this:

Act as if It Were Impossible to Fail!

That short sentence is the formula that will allow you to make a complete about-face from being a failure to becoming an outstanding success. This does not mean that you will not suffer some temporary defeats along the way; you no doubt will. But a setback does not mean you have lost the war; it only means you have lost one little battle. Every time you try a method that does not work, you will know to cross it off your list and try again using a different approach. Let me tell you now about a man who practiced this rule of acting as if it were impossible to fail and became highly successful as a result.

Joseph P. is president of an internationally known cosmetics company that counts its annual receipts in millions of dollars. But it wasn't always that way. Less then thirty years ago, Joseph was fresh out of college with a sheepskin to prove that he had a degree in chemistry.

He was full of fire and enthusiasm to lick the world. Joseph wanted to come up with a formula that would keep cosmetics from deteriorating and spoiling on the shelf. He had no idea of the odds against him in such a project. Even when warned by wholesale drug houses and cosmetic supply firms that he was tackling a project that many had failed at, Joseph nevertheless set out to do the job. He simply refused to accept the idea of failure and firmly planted the idea of success in his mind.

He used every cent he could spare from his position as a junior chemist with a petroleum refining company to buy laboratory equipment, chemicals, and ingredients for his cosmetic experiments. He would mix a formula and put half in the refrigerator and half in the kitchen window in direct sunlight. He wanted to come up with a foolproof formula that would stand up in any kind of household temperature and any type of treatment.

Nearly two years of hard work went by. One morning somewhere in the twenty-third month, Joseph set experiment number

179 out. And as he did, the thought came to him that the prevention of mold and deterioration was not from some substance outside the formula. The prevention of mold was within the mold itself, and therefore, inside the ingredients of the cosmetic compound.

"From then on, it was easy," Joseph says. "I don't know how many more experiments I conducted, but it didn't matter to me, for I knew I had the answer."

Joseph makes it all sound easy as he tells it today. But he succeeded where others would have given up and failed because he refused to accept temporary defeats as permanent failure. He continued to act as if it were impossible to fail, and he succeeded, for *as you think, so shall you become.*

You, too, can succeed when you *act as if it were impossible to fail.* That statement is the golden key that you can use to lock the door on failure and open the door to successful achievement for yourself. *It's all a matter of attitude.*

MASTERING SALES TECHNIQUES

SOLUTIONS: HOW TO WRITE A PERSUASIVE SALES LETTER

One of the most valuable skills any person can master is the ability to persuade others. For salespeople, it is absolutely crucial. When it comes to using the written word to persuade, writing convincing sales letters, there are two major concepts to keep in mind: Power words and hooks.

How to use power words to get your readers to take the action you want them to take.

By carefully observing people, you can learn which words are the best for creating a favorable reaction. But that takes time and experience, so let me give you a head start.

Some words make people think rationally, using logic and reason. Other words cause them to react emotionally. Here is a specific example.

A sharp real estate agent will tell the owner he'll be glad to sell his *house*. He never uses the word *home* when talking with the owner. Home is an emotional word, and the seller can become reluctant to part with his *home* even though he's perfectly willing to get rid of his *house.* By the same token, the real estate agent never sells the buyer a *house.* He always offers him a *home.*

These two words represent two entirely different ideas for the same object. A house is not a home, it's only a house. It's made of bricks, wood, and concrete. It's a very nonemotional idea. But a home is where your heart is, where your family lives, where your kids grow up. It is an extremely emotional power word.

Emotional words are power words, and people are ruled more by emotion than by logic and reason. Salespeople always like to use emotional words because these words cause people to buy. A top salesperson will never ask a person what he *thinks* about a product. Instead, she'll ask her prospect how he *feels* about it.

Think is a nonemotional word that requires a person to use logic and reason. But *feel* is an emotional word that goes straight to the heart, and *the head never hears 'til the heart has listened.*

Power words do more than sell products. You can use them to sell yourself and your ideas. For example, learn which words turn your boss on and which ones turn him off, for no matter what they are, these are power words, too. Everyone has certain likes and dislikes when it comes to language, so you'd be smart to use those "pet" words your boss likes to hear. People like to hear *their* favorite words and phrases played back to them. Emulation is still one of the highest compliments you can pay a person when it is subtly done.

How to use the hook technique in your persuasive sales letters.

To get your reader to take action and do what you want, especially in the convincing type of letter, you must use the *hook technique.* No persuasive sales letter is ever complete without the hook. You may have written a wonderfully interesting letter. You may have captured the reader's interest and even sparked his desire. But if you don't hook him, he won't take the action you want him to take.

Your reader will do what you want him to do for one of two reasons. The first is that you've made him so anxious to get what you've offered, he'll take the required action immediately. But most people tend to procrastinate. They want to think things over for a while. So you must provide another reason to take immediate action. This is where the hook comes in.

You must make the reader understand how she's going to lose out if she doesn't immediately do what you want. The hook presents a penalty if she fails to take action. That is the second reason the reader will do as you ask—*fear.* Unless your hook arouses the fear in her that she will lose something worthwhile if she doesn't act at once, you won't get the results you want.

Fear is on the opposite side of the coin of desire.

If you can't move a person to action by arousing his desire, then you turn the coin over and move him to action by arousing his fear.

For example, I have a letter in front of me right now from the savings and loan association that holds the mortgage on my house. Since my home was bought long before high interest rates, the bank is anxious for me to pay off my loan so they can lend the money out again at a greater interest rate than I'm paying.

They are so anxious for me to do that, they are offering me a discount of several thousand dollars on my present loan if I will pay it off. That's a healthy saving for me and I'm interested, for I'm as eager to save money as anyone else is.

But to make sure I will take action without delay, they closed their letter with a *hook*. Their hook says, "Act now! This offer is for a limited time only and may be withdrawn without any prior notice."

Since the hook technique is usually used in a sales letter where you're trying to persuade someone to do something, I want to give you the exact format you can use.

1. *The opening*. Start by grabbing your readers' attention by fitting in with their train of thought. Establish your point of contact with your readers' self-interests to excite and arouse their curiosity so they will read further into your letter. Remember that everyone wants to know how to make more money or save money.

2. *Cover the benefits to be gained*. Once you have your readers' attention, tell them how they're going to benefit by doing as you ask. Give them a reason to take action. Do this, not only by describing what your product or your proposition is, but also by letting them know what it will do for them. Tell them about the profit, pleasure, convenience, savings in time and labor, and so on that they will gain.

3. *Offer proof of what you say*. The best proof you can offer that your proposition will provide the benefits you've promised is to tell of others who've benefited. Let the readers check with Sam Jones, Sally Brown, or Joe Gray to find out that you're telling the truth.

If you're going to bring in convincing witnesses for testimonials, they must be real people who are willing to let you use their names, addresses, and phone numbers. This requires some extra effort on your part, but there is no better way to gain your prospects' confidence and trust in you and in what you say.

4. *Tell how your readers can gain those benefits*. This is usually done in the next-to-last paragraph. Here you give your readers exact instructions. You tell them exactly what they must do to gain the benefits you've offered.

5. *Close with the hook!* This is the snapper, or the penalty you hold over your reluctant readers. You hook them and force them to take action by telling them about the loss in money or prestige or opportunity that will be theirs if they do not act at once. You normally place the hook in the last paragraph of your letter.

A time penalty is one of the best ways to get the action you want your readers to take. For example: This offer expires in five days; Good only until the fifteenth of March; Prices go up in February; Limited supply, first come, first served; Act now; This offer is for a limited time and may be withdrawn without any prior notice; Four-percent discount good only through the month of November. Even property-tax collectors use this last one.

Let me quickly tell you now the secrets of how to write as you talk so you can get your reader to do what you want:

✔ Make your writing brief.

✔ Take a direct approach.

✔ Break up long sentences into short ones.

✔ Use simple words of one, two, or three syllables so people will be sure to understand you.

✔ Use power words to get your readers to take action. Aim for the heart instead of the head.

✔ Focus your readers' attention on the meaning you want them to get. Leave out unnecessary details.

SOLUTIONS: HOW TO GET PROSPECTS TO PAY IMMEDIATE ATTENTION TO YOU

When you're selling, there are several methods you can use to get a prospect to listen and pay immediate attention to you. For instance, you could use a startling statement, an authoritative quotation, an unusual anecdote, a strong example. However, I prefer using a leading question that promises your listener a benefit, for I believe it is the most effective approach you can use. Here are some quick examples of this potent technique:

✔ How'd you like to make some easy money?

✔ How'd you like to increase profits 25 percent?

✔ How'd you like to double your customers?

✔ How'd you like to cut production costs in half?

✔ Want to get rid of that tired, worn-out feeling?

✔ How'd you like to be proud of your floors?

✔ Want to get more miles per gallon from your car?

No matter what your specific circumstances are, use the kind of question that promises your listeners an immediate benefit just for listening to you. They'll want to give you their full, undivided attention at once.

Not only can you offer your listeners a benefit with the leading question technique, you can also get them saying yes right away, and that's so important in persuading them to do what you want them to do.

When they say yes to your opening question, it establishes a positive mood. This makes it easier for them to continue to agree with you.

Here are nine benefits you can gain by using the leading question technique:

1. *You control the initiative in the conversation.* You actually lead the other person's thinking along the path you want it to take when you ask leading questions. You point her mind in a specific direction so she'll give you the answers that you want.

2. *Leading questions increase your listener's interest.* A person's attention span increases when you can get him to talk by asking him leading questions. The more he talks, the more you learn about him and about what he wants most of all.

3. *When you ask questions, you stimulate a person's thinking.* Questions make your listener more alert and attentive to what you say. She becomes eager to learn more. Many times, your idea becomes her idea and she wants to take credit for it.

I've seen managers and supervisors use questions time and again to get what they wanted by letting the other person think it was all her own idea in the first place.

4. *Questions help reveal your listener's attitude.* When you know what a person's thinking is and what his innermost feelings are, you can slant your approach to meet his individual needs.

5. *Questions let you know whether or not you're getting your point across.* Attention is always lost when the listener doesn't understand what you're trying to say. One of the best ways to find out whether or not your listener is following you is to ask her questions.

Her answers will let you know how good your conversational methods and techniques are. At the same time, her answers will indicate where your approach needs to be improved.

6. *You can reinforce and emphasize major points.* Retention of major points of emphasis is made easier by frequent repetition. When you ask questions on a specific point, it is plain to see that you are stressing that idea. Your listener's answers will reinforce those major points.

7. *Questions make the person feel important.* When you ask questions, you give a person a chance to express his own opinions. That makes him feel important and fulfills one of his basic desires by feeding his ego. When he knows that you are interested in what he says, and that you respect his opinions and ideas, then he'll respect your opinions and ideas, too.

8. *Questions help a person recognize what she actually wants*. When you help a person discover what she actually wants most of all, you'll be in complete control of the conversation. She'll do what you ask as long as she knows she will get what she wants as a result of that action.

9. *Questions help you to find a person's most vulnerable point*. Your listener's weakest spot is your main key to success in persuasion. When you find his most vulnerable point, don't hesitate. Concentrate on it; exploit it immediately. You can use it to get your way every single time.

If you want to find out exactly what your listener wants most of all—if you want to know precisely how you can help him get what he wants so that you, too, will benefit as well—the only sure way to do this is to ask questions, questions, and still more questions.

When you get in the habit of constantly asking questions instead of talking just to hear the sound of your own voice, you'll find that your conversations flow more smoothly, and that's much more exciting and stimulating. Not only that, you'll discover it's highly profitable to you as well.

Asking leading questions that promise a benefit, then, is the surest way of getting a person to pay close attention to you. Questions, rather than statements, can be the most effective way to make a sale, win a person over to your way of thinking, and persuade him to do what you want him to do.

Start with questions that are easy to answer so your listener will relax and feel at ease when he talks with you. People enjoy giving answers they know are right, for it gives them a chance to show how much they know, and that makes them feel important.

This is especially true if your listener is a stranger and you want to sell him something—say, a house or a car. He'll really be on his guard with you in the beginning. Mistrust is characteristic of most of us when we're doing business with someone we don't know.

Your listener doesn't know whether it will be hard or easy to talk with you. The first few things you say will help him decide. As Elmer Wheeler (who was often called America's number one salesman and whose "Sizzlesmanship" methods have been used by most of the country's top corporations) always said, the first ten words were more important than the next ten thousand.

If you're hard to talk with, your listener will become evasive and withdrawn. When you press harder to make your point or close your sale, he'll withdraw even more. This becomes a vicious cycle that ends up with no agreement at all or with a "no sale" sign on the cash register.

But if you start out with easy questions, his nervousness and fear of you will soon disappear. He'll answer your questions with confidence. You ask him more easy questions. He relaxes even more. Soon you're engaged in a pleasant, fruitful, and beneficial conversation.

For instance, a lawyer never presses the witness for an answer to the crucial question the very first thing. A real estate salesperson asks first about the number of children, what kind of house the prospect lives in now, how long it takes him to get to work, whether he prefers living in the city—that sort of thing.

A personnel manager interviewing a job applicant asks questions about a man's family, hobbies, likes and dislikes to put him totally at ease before he starts digging for hard facts about education, past experience, and other business qualifications.

You, too, have to warm up your listener first. You can't approach him with the bureaucratic iciness of an IRS agent and expect him to cotton to you just like that. So just relax and be comfortable. Make it easy for both of you and you'll be able to get what you want.

SOLUTIONS: HOW TO OVERCOME ANOTHER PERSON'S RESISTANCE

Brian Hodge, a highly successful life insurance salesman, kept a record of hundreds of interviews to find out why people bought or failed to buy insurance from him. He found that in more than 85 percent of the cases, the original objection raised by the prospect against buying insurance was not the real reason at all.

Brian found from his research that a person usually had two distinct reasons for not buying life insurance: *one reason that sounds good to the listener and the real reason that he keeps hidden all to himself.*

Brian learned that to find the real reason behind a person's refusal to buy insurance, he had to keep asking one of two simple questions: "Is there any other reason?" or "And in addition to that?"

According to Brian, you must always find that "hidden," or real, reason behind your listener's objections to buying your product or your service. He says that the only way to do that is simply to ask one of those questions or something along the same lines, and keep asking it until you get the answer you need.

If you are persistent enough, Brian says, the real reason will eventually come to the surface. "Usually, you'll hear comments something like this: 'Well, to tell you the truth,' or 'Well, if you really want to know why.' When you hear phrases like these, you'll know that the real objection to buying is coming next. The moment you know the real reason for the person's resistance, you'll know what to do to convert a reluctant prospect into a solid customer."

In addition to Brian's strategy, there is still another excellent technique you can use when you want to get information, not only from a prospective client or customer, but also from other people such as the members of your own family or from your employees or associates.

The most powerful word in the English language for gaining information is a simple three-letter one: *Why?* You can use this little word to keep the other person talking so you can learn what you want to know from him. Let me give you an example now so I can show you how well this technique works:

A friend of mine, Grant Reagan, for years now has told me that he didn't believe in life insurance. So I was really surprised the other day when he said he'd bought a $100,000 policy from a young man the week before. When I asked him how in the world this could have happened, here's what he told me:

"When this young man came calling on me, Jim, I told him I didn't believe in life insurance," Grant said. "But instead of arguing with me as all the other salesmen had done before, he simply looked me straight in the eye and asked, 'Why?'

"Well, I explained to him why, but every time I stopped for breath, he'd ask, 'Why?' and the more I talked, the more I realized there was something wrong with my reasoning. Finally, I convinced myself that he was right and that I was wrong, so I bought some insurance from him.

"Actually, the young man didn't sell me anything. He just kept asking me 'Why?' I sold myself and he made the profit. Smartest salesman I've ever met."

As I've said, you don't need to be in business or in sales to use this highly effective "Why?" technique. You can use it in church, PTA, your club or lodge, or in any other social activity to persuade people to your way of thinking. It will work; I can assure you of that.

So use this "Why?" technique yourself the next time you want someone to do something and they're hesitant at first. They'll usually end up convincing themselves that what you're asking is the right thing for them to do.

SOLUTIONS: THREE SECRETS OF SUCCESSFUL SALESPEOPLE

Although there are a variety of techniques that super salespeople use to become highly successful, they will all agree that these three are without a doubt the most important ones. This first one they place right at the top of the list.

1. *Get your prospect saying Yes immediately.* Leah Brooks, a highly successful mutual fund saleswoman, says that it's extremely important to get your prospective client to say yes immediately.

"I word all my initial questions to a new prospect so the only possible answer he or she can give me is yes," Leah says. "For instance, I might say, 'Would you like to have your investment risk reduced to the absolute minimum?' Of course, the answer always has to be yes. How could it be anything else? Then I follow up my first question with, 'If I can show you how you can gain the maximum return on your investment along with that minimum risk, would you be interested?' Again, the answer has to be yes.

"You can use many other ways to phrase your questions to ensure getting a yes answer. The important thing is getting the prospect saying yes so continually that when the final buying decision has to be made, the word yes just falls out of his or her mouth automatically."

You, too, can use this same technique on your spouse, your children, your friends and associates, anyone. Just get the other person to say yes at the beginning. Keep him from saying no by the way you word your questions.

Why is this technique so successful? A yes answer establishes not only the right psychological frame of mind, but also the proper physiological conditions in the body. All the body processes, both physical and mental, are in an accepting, relaxed, and open attitude when a person says yes.

By the same token, just one single no changes all these psychological and physiological processes into a fighting and defiant mood of rejection. All the body's systems—glandular, muscular, neurological—prepare for a fight. If your wife or husband, your children, a prospective client or customer, or your boss says no to you at the very beginning, it requires a near miracle to change that person's negative attitude to a positive one.

So plan your approach to get an affirmative answer from the other person at the start of your conversation. If you want to win people over to your way of thinking, or if you want to make a sale, then get the other person to agree with you immediately. You'll find that your powers of persuasion increase dramatically when you do. This technique is one of the trade secrets of super salespeople.

2. *The second secret of super salespeople is perseverance.* A characteristic of the top-notch salesperson is to keep coming back time after time even though the prospect continually says no!

One study in salesmanship found that 80 percent of the sales were made after the fifth call on the prospect. After the first call, 48 percent of salespeople quit, 30 percent quit after the second call, 12 percent quit after the third call, but 10 percent keep calling and make 80 percent of the sales. Perseverance pays off.

"How many times do you call on a person before you finally give him up?" I once asked Mark Anderson, a top-notch hardware salesman out of Orlando, Florida.

"It depends on which one of us dies first," Mark said.

Mark then went on to tell me that if he is convinced a prospect is worth calling on, he will keep calling as long as that person is there. "I once made 11 calls on one man before he ever gave me an order," Mark said. "Finally, he told me that he could not keep from buying from me. When I asked him why he said that, he replied, 'Your persistence has paralyzed my resistance!'"

You can use the same technique to get results, too. Just keep calling until you get what you want. Sooner or later your persistence will paralyze your listener's resistance, too.

3. *The third technique is the best way to clinch a sale.* This procedure will work like magic for you whenever there is paperwork to be signed. If no written contract is required, make one up anyway.

Have the contract or order form all ready with your prospect's name, address, the amount to be paid. Every single thing must be completed so all the individual needs to do is sign his name.

When the person starts telling you all the reasons he cannot accept your proposition, don't argue with him. And don't fold up your tent and walk away. Just hand him your pen and point out the big X where his signature goes.

Do you think this method is too presumptuous? Well, it isn't. You'll be glad to find out that you'll never make anyone angry by using this procedure. The magic of this technique is that you focus the person's mind on signing—not on refusing.

You crowd out all the reasons he thinks he should not buy until his mind becomes filled with all the reasons that he should buy. His thoughts then will tend to be translated into positive action.

SOLUTIONS: HOW TO SAVE TIME BY SELLING THE RIGHT PERSON

You'll save much time when you concentrate your selling efforts on the right person. Time is important to all of us. If that's not true, why is it that I see so many drivers going down the road with one hand on the steering wheel and the other hand holding a cellular phone?

Time is a successful salesperson's most valuable asset. She'll never waste it by giving her sales pitch to someone who can't make the buying decision. There's a saying among successful salespeople that goes like this: *Sell the secretary on seeing the boss; sell the boss on buying your product.*

There are some exceptions to this rule, of course, just as there are exceptions to any rule. For instance, if the secretary is going to use the equipment you're selling, then get her on your side first. Sell her on that new computer and then let her sell her boss. Here is one specific example of that technique:

"I called on this particular company only to find that the boss was sick and not in the office that day," Walter Bailey, a young office equipment salesman, told me. "So rather than waste the trip entirely, I demonstrated our new computer to his secretary so she could learn its advantages for herself since she'd be the one using it.

"Later on when I called back, the boss told me he had already reached a tentative agreement with another company.

"'But your secretary knows that our computer will save her time and energy and turn out better work than any other,' I told him. 'Please ask her for yourself. Not only that, our computer is very competitive pricewise with any other and I know I can offer you a sizeable discount if you decide to do all your office equipment business with us.'

"So he called in his secretary for verification of my remarks. She was so enthusiastic in her endorsement that he forgot all about his previous tentative agreement with a different company and bought six new computers from me."

This technique works in other situations as well. For instance, when I got married more than fifty years ago, it was still the custom to introduce the prospective in-laws to each other on some pleasant Sunday afternoon so they could size each other up and find out about their religion, their politics, their drinking habits, and their economic and social status.

On one such occasion when my future in-laws were meeting my parents for the first time, my mother took me aside in the kitchen and said, "You're trying to sell the wrong person, son. Her mother's already sold on you. You don't have to persuade her any longer. Now go after her father. He's the one you need to convince, for he makes all the decisions in that house. She just came along for the ride."

To sum up this idea, then, let me conclude by saying don't waste your time trying to sell your product or service to someone who can't make the buying decision. Save time by selling the person who has the authority to make the decision.

SOLUTIONS: HOW TO CONVINCE PEOPLE THEY WANT WHAT YOU'RE SELLING

Many times, successful selling depends on getting people to recognize their own needs and desires. Onece you convince them that they want what you have to sell, the rest is easy. Not only is this an important secret of selling success, it is also a key rule in all people relationships. I want to give you an example here of how this principle can be used in all walks of life, social as well as business. I am indebted to Leonard Curtis for telling me this story.

"A few years ago, I was elected superintendent of our church Sunday School," Leonard told me. "I felt the immediate need of our church school was for a larger teaching organization so I asked our minister to give me ten minutes to talk to the congregation before our Sunday morning services.

"Now I could've stood up and complained that this job of superintendent had been shoved off on me—after all, I'd heard that complaint many times from previous holders of that office—but I didn't do that. I knew I'd have a far better chance of getting what I wanted from the congregation if I talked to them about the things they wanted from the church for their children. So here's basically what I said to them:

"'I want to talk to you for a few moments about some of the things you want for your children. You want them to come here to Sunday School where they can meet other good children and learn more about life from the truths in this great Book. You and I want our children to keep from making some of the mistakes that we have made. Now how can we do this?

"'First of all, we need a larger teaching staff. We now have only six teachers for our Sunday School classes. We need at least twelve. Some of you may hesitate to teach because you feel you don't know enough about the Bible. I felt the same way when I took over a class a year ago. But let me tell you this: You'll learn more about the Bible in six months by teaching the children for thirty minutes or so each Sunday morning than you'll ever learn in six years by just reading it all by yourselves.

"'You husbands and wives can study and prepare the Sunday School lessons together. It will give you something more to do in common besides watching television. And it'll bring you a lot closer together than those TV programs ever will. When your children see you taking an active interest in church programs, they'll become more interested, too. I don't know of any better way to improve and multiply your talents than through this wonderful work of teaching a child how to live a better life. And I know that is exactly what you want for your children, a better life than you have had.'

"Do you know what happened? Well, we got eleven new teachers that morning, five more than I'd asked for! In fact, we had more teachers than there were children to go around at first, So we started a house-to-house canvass in our neighborhood to invite more children to our Sunday School classes. After the children started coming, their parents began to follow. We soon reached the point where our original building was full and overflowing, so last year we built a brand-new church building. All this from talking to people for ten minutes about what they wanted most of all and then showing them how they could get it."

So please remember this principle: People don't always know what they really want, but once you show it to them they'll recognize it. If you follow this basic rule, it will solve all your people problems for you, including the ones in your own family.

PRESENTING YOURSELF IN THE BEST LIGHT

SOLUTIONS: HOW TO TALK AND ACT IN A MEETING

Your actions in a meeting will depend a great deal on whether you're in charge of the meeting or whether you're merely a participant. I'd like to give you some tips on how to conduct yourself if you're one of the people in attendance.

When you're attending a meeting as a participant, be prepared for it. Some meetings are routine, like weekly sales and supervisory meetings or staff conferences. Even so, it's still a wise idea to drop by the office of your boss's assistant the day before and find out if anything special is going to be taken up this week.

This is a healthy procedure to follow even for those routine meetings, so you can always be ready to answer your boss's questions. But if he's called a special meeting for some reason, then it's critical for you to find out what's on the agenda.

And speaking of special meetings with the boss, *especially if you're the only one invited,* I've learned something else during my long years of experience in business, industry, and the armed services that holds true 98 percent of the time.

If the boss calls and says he'd like to get together with you this afternoon *in your office*— no problem; don't worry about it. Very few people have ever gotten the axe in their own office. A boss likes to be sitting behind his own desk when he has to take punitive action of some sort. That desk is his symbol of authority.

But if he calls you and tells you to *be in his office* at two sharp this afternoon, you'd better think twice and try to find out what's really going on. Could be the roof might be just about ready to cave in on top of you.

My point is that where that meeting is being held and who's attending it can be a major clue as to just how important it is.

Be on time.

I know of no other single thing that can so easily make you appear to be careless, negligent, and inefficient to your boss than being late to her meetings.

This might be the only time she sees you during the week, so you want to be sure you make a good impression on her. Being on time is an easy way to do that and to put yourself across favorably with her.

But if you're always late, she'll start wondering if you run your own department in the same slipshod manner. She's bound to have some doubts about you and your operation.

A small point, perhaps, but it can become a big one in your boss's eye. If you want to be known as a reliable person who can always be depended on to get the job done, then always be on time.

Don't ask questions that waste other people's time.

If you have a question that's going to affect most of the people in the meeting, then ask it by all means. If it's a question that could change current policies and procedures for everyone, then every person there should know the answer, of course.

But if your boss's answer is going to affect only you or your operation, then it would be far better to take it up with him after the meeting on an individual basis. Most employers leave an opportunity at the end of a meeting so that individual problems can be resolved without wasting everyone else's time.

Contribute what you can to make the meeting a success.

You may not like to attend meetings any more than I do. When I was in the army many years ago, I used to wonder how the regimental commander expected us to get our work done, for we were constantly being called to attend one of his innumerable staff meetings.

Maybe you feel that way sometimes, too, but if you're a junior executive in the company, you'll need to cooperate with your boss for your own benefit, so you might as well do it willingly and cheerfully.

One of the best ways you can show your willingness to cooperate with your boss is to contribute your ideas during meetings. The person who takes the lead in offering practical suggestions and logical solutions to problems at a staff conference will be looked on by the boss as a dependable and valuable associate: the right kind of person to have around when the going gets tough.

If you're that kind of person, you'll soon be marked for promotion. You'll be given a helping hand up the management ladder, for your ideas will come to be respected. Just make sure your contributions are sensible and worthwhile.

If you don't understand, say so.

Don't be afraid to ask a question if you don't understand something. It's better to ask for clarification so you can do the job right than not to ask and end up doing it wrong.

SOLUTIONS: HOW TO CONDUCT A MEETING IF YOU'RE IN CHARGE

I just showed you how to talk and act as a participant in someone else's meeting. Now I'm going to give you tips on how to conduct your own meetings:

Introduce new people.

This not only makes for good fellowship, but it also makes it easier for people to interact without any inhibitions. If a lot of people attend your meetings, have them wear a slip of paper with their name on it pinned to the breast pocket of their coat or shirt.

One of the features I did like about the army was its policy of having everyone wear name tags. This simple procedure saved a lot of us all sorts of embarrassment at times when we couldn't remember someone's name.

Have your exhibits ready.

If you have exhibits to show, make sure they're ready. If you're using charts, make certain that an easel or an A-frame is available and that your charts will turn easily. Nothing can be more disconcerting during a meeting than to have some of your exhibits missing, out of order, or stuck together.

Start your meeting on time.

Just because you're in charge of the meeting doesn't mean that you should have any special privileges on this point. If you personally are paying your subordinates, I'm sure you won't want them sitting idly on their hands waiting for you. They can't make money for you that way.

And even if you're not paying them yourself but are a supervisor, a manager, or an executive of some sort in the company, that's still no excuse for you to be late. No matter how high you are in your organization, someone will still be keeping tabs on you, too.

If a record should be kept, appoint someone to do so.

Normally speaking, if a meeting is worth holding, then it ought to be worth recording it.

You could have your secretary record the minutes of your meeting or use a tape recorder to do so. Show when and where it was held, who was present, what was discussed, and what decisions were made.

After your meeting is over, have the notes typed up, okay them for reproduction, and send mimeographed or reproduced copies *within twenty-four hours* to all the people who attended your meeting. This procedure will keep them from making mistakes because of some point they misunderstood during the meeting.

Don't discuss personal matters with individuals.

If you want to discuss a sales problem with your sales manager, don't waste your warehouse foreman's time unless it's going to affect his operation. Every section or department will have unique problems not common to all. It's best to handle those with the concerned persons on an individual basis.

Summarize the highlights.

Before you close your meeting, it's best to again emphasize the major points you have disucssed. The basic format for your meetings should be: (1) Tell them what you're going to tell them; (2) tell them; (3) tell them what you've told them.

Don't hold a meeting unless it's necessary.

This has always been one of my pet peeves against the armed services, business, and industry. I've attended all kinds of weekly staff conferences where nothing new was discussed. Why was the meeting held? Out of pure habit—nothing else.

So if you want to stop wasting your employees' time and your money, then don't hold a meeting just for the sake of holding a meeting. As an Episcopalian minister, Bishop Emrich from Michigan, once said, "To do that is to use about the same kind of logic a church group uses when it meets in order to raise money to meet the budget in order that they might have a place to meet to raise money to meet the budget!"

SOLUTIONS: HOW TO SPEAK AT EMPLOYEES' EVENTS

Good employee relations are important in every company. Satisfactory human relations must be established inside the organization before you can ever hope to have good public relations on the outside with customers and clients.

There are likely to be all kinds of opportunities in your company to hold special affairs or celebrations that will be attended by most of your employees. Many times you will be asked to speak. Talks like these should be handled very carefully.

Don't look at them as distasteful or a waste of time or unnecessary. You can use these occasions as splendid opportunities to put yourself and your company across with your employees. Everything you can do to promote better employee-management relations in your company is an important part of your job.

"*You should invent opportunities to improve human relations in your company,*" says Fred Justice, director of public relations for a huge electronics manufacturing company in Florida. "The number of such affairs you have throughout the year will depend entirely on how much you want to make out of it. It's entirely up to you.

"For instance, you could honor certain employees for length of service, using a five-year period as a basis. If you honored people for every five years of consecutive service up through twenty-five years, that would give you at least five different occasions to speak to almost everyone in your company.

"And you don't have to limit such special occasions only to celebrations of years of service or retirement. You can hold a special function when someone gets married, especially if they both work for you; if someone is celebrating an important anniversary; if someone returns from service in the armed forces; or if someone has performed some especially meritorious feat that is worthy of special recognition.

"Whatever the reason for the special occasion, you can make it an affair that gives everyone a chance to get into the act. These events help bring everyone in your organization closer together. They establish a feeling of unity and harmony between you and your employees."

For instance, here's an outline you can follow for an after-dinner speech to celebrate the safe return of one of your people from the armed forces:

1. Offer congratulations on a safe return to family and loved ones.

2. Mention some significant aspect of military service: awards, decorations, service medals, promotions, and so on.

3. Offer a warm welcome back into the company.

4. Talk about his or her previous excellent service with you. Tell of some previous contributions to the company.

5. Wish the person the best of luck and express your personal desires for continued success with your organization.

Now let's look at an outline you can use for celebrating a person's length of service with your company:

1. Extend your own personal congratulations.

2. Feature the fact that she has come up through the ranks; mention some of her previous jobs and responsibilities.

3. Recall some of her earlier days with the company.

4. Stress her personal development: character, industry, reliability, resourcefulness, cooperativeness, and so on.

5. Mention some well-known aspect of her present work that is worthy of special praise and attention.

6. Describe how the company has benefited from her long years of faithful service.

7. Tell some of the good things her co-workers say about her today.

8. Offer congratulations on behalf of both the company and your employees.

9. Present her with a suitable gift or service award.

10. Express your personal wishes for many more happy and useful years ahead, whether she's retiring from your company or staying on with you.

Now just another thought or two about these functions for length of service. During the earlier years, it might be best to honor groups of people and speak in more general terms about all of them at the same time.

But when a faithful employee has attained many years of loyal service, then it would be far more appropriate to honor him or her on an individual basis rather than in a group.

SOLUTIONS: HOW TO GIVE A VIP BRIEFING

In the old days, only heads of state, high-ranking government officials such as senators and cabinet members, generals, admirals, persidents of corporations, and chairmen of boards of directors rated VIP (very important person) briefings.

Today, however, because of the enormous volume of technical information and statistical data needed just to keep up with current developments, average corporation executives, plant managers, and business people all have to depend on briefings by their subordinates—junior executives, foremen, supervisors, department heads—to keep themselves fully informed and up to date.

So no matter how junior you are in the organization, sooner or later you'll have to give a briefing to someone ranked higher than you. VIP briefings are here to stay.

A VIP briefing, however, is not used to persuade or to get a person to take some action or make a decision. It is not used to impress or convince your listener of anything. Nor is it meant to entertain the VIP. *A VIP briefing should be used only to inform.*

You can look at a VIP briefing as a way of giving up-to-date information about your own operation to someone who is either your senior or your superior.

GUIDELINES FOR A VIP BRIEFING

✔ *Restrict your subject to fit the time.* If you've been given only half an hour to talk, but you think you need an hour to tell about your entire operation, then something has to give—either your time or your subject.

Since the time of your VIP is so limited—that's why he or she has to resort to briefings in the first place—chances are you'll have to condense your talk and *cover only the major points of interest about your operation.*

Stick to just a few major points and cover them well rather than try to cover everything and leave nothing but a blurred, vague impression of confusion in your listener's mind. Later on, though he may not remember your name or your face, he'll think of you as "that person who was so confused that he didn't seem to know what was really going on in his own department."

✔ *Arrange your ideas in a logical sequence.* Almost all topics can be developed logically by using a time or procedure sequence. In the time sequence, for instance, you could treat your subject from the viewpoint of past, present, and future. Or you could begin at a specific date and go forward or backward from there.

"A procedure sequence is especially useful in industrial briefings," says Tim Kelly, production superintendent with a large Pennsylvania steel company. "It begins with the raw material stage and moves through each step of the manufacturing process until the finished product is reached.

"If you were in charge of a production line, for instance, you could brief your visitors by starting with the smaller component parts and moving down the line to your final assembly point."

✔ *Number your points as you make them.* One of the best ways to keep your briefing neat and clean and to show you know what you're talking about is to enumerate your principal points of interest. Be specific about doing this; there's no need to be vague about it. Simply say it this way: "My first point is . . . the second thing I want to talk about is . . . third, I want to consider . . . last, I want to say . . . " You'll be remembered as a person who really knows the business.

✔ *Compare the unfamiliar with the familiar.* Remember that when you're briefing someone about your operation, you're the expert—no matter how many degrees the person might have or what his or her position is. What might be quite ordinary and commonplace to you might seem extremely strange and complex to the VIP.

If your field is computers, for example, don't expect the corporation president to be a programmer. Always remember that executives work with people—not things. If you're going to discuss computer programming, compare that with something familiar—something readily understandable—like driving a car.

✔ *Avoid technical terms.* You might be briefing the chairman of the board, but that doesn't mean he or she understands the exact technical terms of your department.

"I once watched a brilliant young chemist in the research and development department of a cosmetic firm brief the corporation president," Donald Baird, an executive with Universal Laboratories in Atlanta, Georgia, told me. "He wanted to show his listener how much he knew and how important his job was.

"So he used *every* technical word he could think of to impress his boss, although he normally translated his highly technical and scientific terminology into common words for the men and women who worked in the compound room and on the mixing tanks.

"Unfortunately, the president thought he was trying to make a fool of him, so a week later he summarily fired him. 'If that young man tried to make a fool out of me with his big vocabulary and college degree, think how much more he'd try to make fools out of the people in the plant,' he said. 'We can't afford to have his smart-alecky kind around. There are plenty more chemists where he came from!'"

An unfortunate situation, without a doubt. The thing is, you don't talk down to corporation presidents, whether or not that is your intention.

✔ *Use visual aids.* Even VIPs enjoy visual aids. It's the fastest way to transmit information and it saves time. So use them. Your listeners will appreciate you and your efforts when you do.

Now a VIP briefing is different from any other kind of lecture or talk you'll ever give. Being so unique, it also has some distinctive pointers or briefing tips to keep in mind:

1. ***Don't summarize a VIP briefing.*** A VIP briefing is in a sense a summary in itself. It should be an abridgement or a synopsis of your operation. Your listener assumes that you've included only those major points of interest she should know. The restatement of those major points is not at all fitting for a briefing audience.

2. ***Don't ask questions.*** The idea of using questions to check an audience understanding or for any other purpose is entirely out of place here. Whatever you do, don't insult the intelligence of your listeners.

3. ***Don't emotionalize.*** Remember the purpose of a VIP briefing. You're not giving a talk to persuade or get action or a decision. You are not trying to impress or convince anyone of anything. Nor are you trying to entertain. *A VIP briefing should be used only to inform.*

4. **Be factual.** Your briefing must be an unbiased presentation of the facts and only the facts. No coloring or shading is permitted.

5. **Don't tell your listener something she already knows.** You are briefing the VIP to tell her what she doesn't know, so never use the phrase, "As you know . . . ."

I can remember when a new general took over the command of an army post in Missouri. He sent out the word through his chief of staff that he didn't want to hear the words *General, as you know.* "If I already know," he said, "then don't waste my time by telling me again." Unfortunately, his words fell upon some deaf ears, which soon burned and turned red from the general's comments!

6. **Be formal.** This idea may sound strange to you, but remember you're briefing very important people. I don't mean your briefing should be stuffy and dull or rigid and inflexible. Nor do I mean that you should use four- and five-syllable words or pompous and cumbersome verbiage.

I do mean you should not assume a casual or highly informal attitude. Don't use a sweatshirt-and-sneakers approach. Your delivery should be natural and relaxed, yet it should be kept businesslike and systematic.

7. **Be flexible.** Thorough preparation and confidence in yourself give you the ability to react quickly to changes in time schedules, to answer searching questions, and to adjust to a variety of different audiences.

8. **Be brief.** Because your listener's time is so valuable, you must be concise in your presentation and answers to questions.

9. **Don't use a strong closing statement.** Since you are not making a speech to persuade someone to do something, to make a decision and the like, a strong closing statement to get the listener to take action of some sort is not in order. The best way to close is simply to say, "Ladies and gentlemen, this concludes my briefing."

SOLUTIONS: HOW TO BUILD GOOD COMMUNITY CONTACTS FOR YOURSELF

Smart corporation executives and business leaders look for opportunities to take an active part in the affairs of their communities. And they expect their executives and managers to do the same. You can develop goodwill for your company when you build good community contacts for yourself.

Good community relations also help you build your reputation and can help you develop your career. A variety of clubs and organizations are interested in civic and social affairs, education, charity, religion, politics, and business. You should easily be able to find one that appeals to your own personal interests.

"If you're in business for yourself, you have an excellent opportunity to develop good public relations and goodwill for your business when you're working with community groups," says George Latimer, owner of the Latimer Hardware Stores in Orlando and Daytona Beach, Florida.

"Business relations and community relations are dependent upon each other. As you serve your community in one way or another, you will become better known to civic leaders and important people in your city. People tend to do business with someone who's interested in the betterment of his own community."

So spread the good word about yourself by joining clubs and civic organizations in your town. You'll do many interesting things; you'll learn many valuable things and you'll acquire a reputation as an individual who gets things done—a good person to know and with whom to do business.

Be willing to speak at community affairs.

Occasions are bound to come along when you'll be asked to say a few words or to make a short speech at some community event. Whatever you do, don't refuse. This is a splendid opportunity for you to spread yourself even further and make your ideas and suggestions known on a city-wide or larger basis.

"Contrary to what many people think, most politicians don't get into politics just because they're lawyers," says Jack Morse, a former United States congressman from the Midwest. "They get into politics because they're interested in community affairs in their own hometowns.

"They soon learn that if they want to be successful in either politics or community relations, they must know how to talk with people. They must reach the position where their opinions and their ideas can be heard. You can't become a community leader or a politician sitting at home behind closed doors.

"An important point to remember—whether you're on the platform campaigning for office or soliciting money for some charity—is to keep the *we* attitude and the *you* approach. If you start sounding like an individual instead of a member of the group, you're bound to lose a great deal of your group support.

"People want their community leaders, their congressmen and women and their senators to speak *for* them, not *to* them or *about* them. If you talk only as an individual, expressing just your own ideas and your own opinions, people will soon get the impression that you're interested only in yourself and that you're just using them as a tool to get what you want. They'll feel you're seeking some personal advantage instead of a benefit for the entire community."

So follow Jack Morse's advice, even if you're not planning on running for a political office. Talk with people as if you were representing them, as if you were concerned only with their interests rather than your own, and you'll gain their solid backing and strong support.

Do it from the heart.

When you become interested in community affairs, don't do it with tongue in cheek. You'll be as phony as a three-dollar bill if you do. So do it with all your heart. Go all the way.

"When you join a club or an organization in your town, don't stop there," says James Neff, a member of the Junior Chamber of Commerce in the rapidly growing city of Palm Bay, Florida.

"Become an active member of that group. Take part in everything they do. Don't refuse to serve on a committee. Volunteer to help. Don't be shy or afraid to join in. Just because you pay your dues or contribute some token service, that doesn't mean you're really community minded. A person is accepted into an organization not just for the dues he or she pays, but also for the worthwhile services he or she can contribute to the entire group."

So think in terms of not what you can get but what you can give. The more you give, the more you'll get back. That's an irrefutable law of human relations and community affairs.

Giving wholeheartedly is the kind of service that makes you an important member of your community. It builds up your reputation and your good name. When that happens, you can't help but reap benefits for yourself too.

Community service is one of the best ways I know of to win the hearts and minds of people. So pitch in.

WINNING STRATEGIES FOR WOMEN

SOLUTIONS: HOW TO BE A SUCCESSFUL WOMAN IN A MAN'S WORLD

Although most of the problems discussed in this book are written with the idea of being useful to both men and women, the next several are primarily of interest to women.

It may not be fair, but the business world still is primarily male territory. Men still call most of the shots. A woman entering the business world for the first time may suddenly feel as if she's knee-deep in quicksand. Of course, women have made big gains in the business world, and a lot of them have developed extremely successful careers. In fact, *CEO* magazine says that 20 percent of all businesses in this country are owned by women and that this percentage should increase substantially in the years ahead. Unfortunately, when it comes to being given completely equal opportunities, women still have a long way to go.

However, if as a woman you know what you want and are willing to follow the strategies presented here, you can succeed. No one can stop you if you have enough determination and perseverance. I want to give you four techniques that will help you develop a successful career as a woman. I know there are others, but I've been told by some highly successful women that these four are the most important, especially when starting out. (Interestingly enough, all four techniques are just as helpful to men.)

1. *Know exactly what your goal is*. The first step in becoming a successful woman in a man's world is to know exactly what your goal is. This might sound ridiculously simple, yet I have talked to scores of young businesswomen in my *Seminars for Female Executives* who say they want to accomplish great things in business, but they don't have the slightest idea what those great things are. They've set no goals for themselves, they say, because they aren't sure how high they can go as women in a business world that belongs primarily to men.

My answer to that is always the same. You can go as high as your capabilities will take you. If you can do the job, don't limit yourself by creating obstacles and barriers that don't exist except in your own mind.

Determine, then, exactly what specific goal you want to attain. Do you want to be president of your own company some day? Is this your dream? Then dedicate yourself toward achieving that goal with unswerving singleness of purpose.

2. *Give it your best shot*. Once you know what you want, go after it with everything you've got. Going after what you want requires persistence and plain dogged determination, not giving up, not quitting at the first setback. If you've developed your mental and intellectual resources and are ready for the long haul ahead, you'll have sufficient strength to follow up and ensure your continued success.

Tracy Gilmore, the female president of an Atlanta executive placement firm, told me this: "Men in high-ranking management positions are afraid that even the most enthusiastic woman executive will drop everything for the first appealing man who comes along. Marriage is the biggest single reason women will scrap their career plans. When the going gets rough, marriage can look like an easy out."

No doubt about it; marriage can change things. A newly married woman may pay more attention to her husband than she does to her job and her career. But you can be successful at both if you keep your priorities in line.

3. *Learn to get along with your boss*. If you want to get ahead and stay there, you have to get along with your boss. No one is more important to you and your career than the man or woman who can get you promoted or raise your pay.

You'll always get along better with your boss if you're known as a hard worker. Nothing makes a boss happier than the sight of an employee toiling away at the job. Looking busy, sounding busy, and being busy are not only smart office politics, but also simply good business, period.

However, being a good worker is not enough. You must also reinforce and build up your boss's ego and self-image while doing the best job you can. Make sure your styles mesh. If he works at a rapid-fire pace, then give him fast and concise answers—bare facts stated briefly without embellishment. If she enjoys hearing a lot of detail, then give her that. Always follow the boss's lead.

4. *Learn to delegate responsibility*. This is the most distinguishing hallmark of the successful executive. Unfortunately, a common mistake that many female executives make is in not delegating responsibility properly.

Watch the men around you. See how the competent ones do it. Smart male executives will chop up an assignment—no matter how small it already is—and pass various tasks around to their subordinates to do. Even when it might be quicker to do the job themselves, they will not do so.

Women, on the other hand, tend to hang onto every detail of an assignment, even when it's large and complex. They are afraid that if something goes wrong, they'll get all the blame. If you do this, you'll limit your own effectiveness. You'll be passed over for promotion, for it'll be obvious to your superiors that you can't handle anything bigger or higher than what you are doing right now.

So don't hesitate, delegate. Every time you give something to someone else to do, you free yourself to accept more responsibility. Top management is always happy to know there is a capable person around to take care of new assignments. Be smart; let that someone be you.

The three key words for delegating responsibility are "Organize, Deputize, Supervise." First, *organize the work to be done* by breaking it up into smaller pieces. Then, *deputize by passing out those pieces to specific people to do*. Finally, *super-*

vise each individual's work to make sure that it's being done properly and on time. There's no limit to what you can get done if you use this simple technique to delegate responsibility to others.

SOLUTIONS: HOW A WOMAN CAN DEVELOP THE AURA OF POWER

My first recommendation is that as a woman you should not use male power symbols. Judith Phillips, a New York management consultant for female executives, agrees with me. So here are the seven success techniques for women that Judith gave me to help you get started:

1. ***Develop your own self-power attitude***. Self-power must be real. It can't be faked. You must feel it inside yourself generating so strongly that other people will sense it, too. Your self-power must be so forceful that others will not even dare to criticize you or find fault with you. You need fear no challenge, for you are not inferior to anyone.

2. ***Hire a male secretary***. As an executive, you'll be entitled to a secretary, but *don't* hire a woman. Hire a man instead, Judith suggests. This will increase your visible power tremendously.

A man is not likely to doubt your authority when he hears a male secretary's voice on the phone saying, "I'm sorry, but *Ms.* Brown is busy right now and can't speak to you. Would you care to call back?

Never let your secretary say, "May she call you back?" Make sure he always says, "Would you care to call back?" This establishes you as the dominant personality in this power duel. You are clearly the one in control.

3. ***Know where to sit in a staff conference***. Unless you yourself are the boss, the second power position is always to the left of the boss. This is true in both civilian and military circles. There is usually a straight-backed chair at this position. The number two person always sits there. Other seats are normally easy chairs and couches.

Get to the meeting first and sit down in this power seat. If anyone questions your right to sit there, say that you have a back problem and that your chiropractor or your orthopedic doctor insists that you not slump or sit in a soft easy chair.

You'll soon be regarded as a person of power on the way up, second only to the boss. Many a successful career has been started by simply sitting in the right chair.

4. *Know how to handle male visitors in your office.* Chairs for visitors in your office should be easy chairs and a couch or sofa, Judith recommends. When you are sitting in the power position behind your desk and your male visitor is slumped down or sprawled out in an easy chair or sofa, he's immediately at a disadvantage. It's much easier for you to retain the upper hand psychologically when he's slouched down in a weaker position.

If you are this person's superior, you can also choose to stroll around while talking to him, while he cannot do this. You can even place your hands on your hips and spread your feet slightly to visibly project your power.

5. *Challenge someone else's play for power.* Ever stub your toe on a rock and then hurt your foot even worse when you kicked it? The rock is completely silent. It can't talk back or tell you how it happened. No matter how much you yell or kick or swear, it won't say a word.

You can use the rock's tactics on your challenger. Simply ignore him. Say nothing. Pay no attention to his demands, his threats, or his blustering. The quieter you remain, the more flustered he will become. But hold your ground; when you pay no attention to him, he'll finally give up and leave you alone.

6. *Use the "steepling" technique.* I gave you this technique in Problem #8 under the *Solution: How to Read Other People's Body Language and Effectively Use Your Own,* (page 85) so I don't want to repeat it here. But since Judith regards this technique as one of the best you can use to project your power, I would ask that you refer back to it to refresh your memory.

7. *Build yourself some powerful alliances.* Nobody "has it made" in the business or industrial world. Somebody dies, retires, embezzles some funds, becomes an alcoholic, suffers burnout from

overwork, or cracks up with personal problems, a divorce, a child's drug addiction, or whatever.

Any of these things can send shock waves through the entire company, changing the power structure completely. Build some alliances for yourself so you can move in whatever direction the situation dictates.

SOLUTIONS: HOW A SECRETARY CLIMBED HER WAY TO SUCCESS IN A BIG COMPANY

The first thing you must realize as a secretary is that *no one is interested in your success but you and you alone.* In fact, your boss probably is the last person in the entire company who wants to see you get ahead because he doesn't want to lose you. If he loses you, he has to start all over again, educating and training a new secretary to do the work the way he wants it done.

Now here are six techniques you can use to climb the executive ladder to success in the big company:

1. *Attract the attention of the upper hierarchy.* Although you do want to keep your boss happy with you and your work, your primary goal must be to get ahead. If you are a secretary, the best way for you to move up the management ladder is to become known to your superior's boss as a knowledgeable and competent person who really understands the intricate workings of the company inside out. Let me show by an example exactly how to do that:

Peggy Gilbert is today the chief administrative officer for a large corporation. She has the title of executive vice-president and reports directly to the president of the company. She has a large staff of her own to carry out her duties. Yet Peggy started out as a file clerk for a department foreman way down on the totem pole.

"I didn't want to be a file clerk all my life, so I formulated my own plan of attack and my own time table for success," Peggy says. "The first thing I knew I had to do was attract the attention of those who really counted. Except for ordinary reports and routine memos, I quickly learned to keep important correspondence and major reports out of the interoffice mail. When I saw that a letter or a report was of significant nature, I would suggest to my boss that I hand carry it to his superior. Of course, I always implied that this would make my own boss look good for his thoughtfulness.

"Once in his superior's office, I would bypass his secretary by saying, 'Mr. Bell asked me to personally give this report to Mr. Howard.' I wouldn't just lay it down on Mr. Howard's desk and leave. Instead, I would hand it to him and say, 'This is the report on production you've been waiting for from Mr. Bell. I'll be glad to stay for a moment so I can answer any questions you might have.'

"I always made it very clear that I understood the report and that I knew what it was all about. Before long, Mr. Howard got in the habit of telling his own secretary to 'Call Peggy and ask her; she'll know.' When his own secretary got married and left, he didn't look around to find a replacement. He immediately tagged me and I took my first step up the executive ladder.

"I didn't stay long in Mr. Howard's office. That was only an intermediate goal. I used the same process, with a few variations, to become vice president in charge of all administration."

I myself used this same technique successfully when I was in the army during World War II. I was a sergeant. My boss was a major. As a regimental staff officer, he attended weekly division staff meetings. Since he was hard of hearing, he almost always came back with unintelligible notes. I suggested that I attend the meetings with him and take notes.

High-ranking division officers got used to seeing a sergeant come with the major to take notes and answer questions. One day the Commanding General attended the meeting. He watched me closely and asked several other officers why I was there. After the meeting was over, I was directed to report to his office.

"You shouldn't be an enlisted man," he told me. "You should be an officer. You're already performing the duties of a major, but you're only receiving the pay of a sergeant. I'm recommending you immediately for a field promotion to a first lieutenant."

Thirty days later, I was commissioned an officer in the United States Army without having to endure the physical and mental stress of thirteen weeks of Infantry Officer Candidate School. Not only that, I received my commission as a first lieutenant. Had I gone to Officer Candidate School, I would have been commissioned one grade lower as a second lieutenant.

2. *Become the fountainhead of information and knowl-edge*. Just as Peggy did, you will attract the attention of the people who count when you fill yourself with accurate and useful information. The more knowledge you display, the more often people will turn to you to find out what they need to know.

The more information you gain about the entire operation, that much more will your boss depend on you for answers. It will soon reach the point where he won't go to a staff meeting without you. When he turns to you for an answer when the company president asks him a question, your name is going to be remembered.

3. *Never come early, but always stay late*. If you show up early, the only people who'll ever see you are the janitor or the security guard. Neither one of them can help you get promoted.

Never, and I repeat never, leave before your boss does. If you do, that will be the day he'll want to ask you something. If he gets the answer he needs from someone else, you will lose some luster in his eyes. So always, and again I repeat, always, leave after your boss does. He'll be impressed with your loyalty to the company and your devotion to duty.

If possible, time your departure with that of *his* boss. The more his boss sees you, the more he'll remember you. Carry some trade journals so he can see how interested you are in your profession. But don't carry anything that suggests you're doing your work at home. This would give him the impression that you're not efficient enough to get your work done during normal office hours.

4. *Eat your lunch at your desk*. You don't have to do this every day; several times a week will do. This also implies great devotion to duty and creates a good impression. But don't read a newspaper or magazine or do your face or nails at your desk during the lunch hour. This spoils the effect you're trying to create. Instead, open a file or a report. If your boss wants to know why you're not going out to lunch, tell him you want to absorb the details of this complicated report while everyone's gone and it's peaceful and quiet.

Don't worry that people will think you're cheap or antisocial when you brown bag it. You're in good company when you do. Leon Peters, former chairman of the board of Cushman and Wakefield Realtors and consultant to RCA, did this, and so do many other top executives. They can get much of their most important work done when most of the office staff is out and there isn't much chance for telephone interruptions.

5. ***Look as if you were already a top-level executive.*** I'm not going to go into the details of how you should dress. That depends on where you live and what the dress code and customs are for your company. The important thing is for you to show those above you that you will fit in perfectly well at their level.

6. ***If you can't go up vertically, move laterally.*** It will sometimes happen that no matter what you do, you won't be able to move up where you are. In that case, move laterally from one job to another. You'll not only learn more about the company, but you will sooner or later find the right slot where you can move up the ladder.

If anyone higher up wonders about your horizontal movements, you can always say that you want to get the broadest education possible about all departments in the company so you'll be better qualified. This always impresses the hierarchy. They'll remember your name when the right time comes.

SOLUTIONS: HOW A WOMAN CAN SUCCEED IN HER OWN BUSINESS

Today, women are increasingly earning the right to position, power, and equality in large companies and corporations. And 20 percent of all businesses in this country are owned by a woman, as I mentioned earlier.

I want to give you some examples of successful women I am personally familiar with so you can see for yourself how you, too, can be a successful woman in your own business if that is what you desire.

First, I want to tell you that often it's the simplest of gadgets that can be the most successful. For example, the little things you and I use every day came about as the result of someone's new idea: the paper clip, which made its inventor a millionaire many times over; the safety pin, which made a fortune for one of the great aristocratic families of the United States; Scotch tape, the stapler, carbon paper. Then there're erasers on the end of pencils. That person also became a millionaire from his idea. The ballpoint pen did the same thing for its inventor. And now, for the latest, the Topsytail!

Tomima Edmark, who invented the Topsytail, became a multi-millionaire from her simple idea. Let me tell you about her amazing success story. In 1989, Tomima was an IBM computer sales-woman. She wore a long blond ponytail that she felt looked a bit dull. She found she could braid her ponytail and make it better looking with a makeshift device made from a plastic loop and a knitting needle.

Her device worked so well for her she wondered if other women could use such a product. Realizing the potential of her new hair gadget, Tomima, then only thirty-two, paid $5,000 to patent her product, which she named Topsytail.

Hoping that companies that sold combs and hair brushes would be interested in her new product, she called on Riviera Trading Corporation and Goody Products. Both of them refused to buy her product.

But Tomima Edmark was a good saleswoman. She was challenged by these refusals and decided to market her Topsytail on her own. Spending $9,000 of her savings for a mold, she located a plastics maker who could produce as many Topsytails as she needed for 50 cents each.

Then she started advertising her product in small hairstyle magazines. The first ad in April 1991 brought in orders worth $1,000. Tomima filled those orders herself, stuffing Topsytails into envelopes each night after her work at IBM. By the end of the year, she was selling 200 Topsytails every week at $10 each.

While she was in New York on IBM business, Tomima persuaded a magazine editor from Glamour magazine to try Topsytail. This editor then featured it in the February 1992 issue. Within three weeks, Tomima had $100,000 worth of orders and had to get her cleaning woman to help her fill 400 orders a week at night.

A few weeks later, she got her biggest break of all, although it did not seem like it at the time: IBM laid her off!

With an early retirement payment of $25,000, Tomima lived off her money while she showed her Topsytail to retailers. In previous trips to trade shows and hair salons with a promotional video, Tomima had found that Topsytail sales increased greatly when women could see how easy it was to use her plastic device. So she began looking for someone to help her get Topsytail on television.

Her strategy worked. In the six months after her first TV commercial, Topsytail sold 3.6 million at $15 each. And when Tomima advertised it on QVC, she sold 5,000 at $15 each in eleven minutes. And it's been reported that Topsytail made over $50 million in the first six months of 1993! As you can plainly see, Topsytail was a simple idea, but it paid off in big results.

Pamela Yardis, the successful founder of Chestnut Hill Consulting Group, a million-dollar-a-year enterprise, says, "You can always talk your way out of doing things. If you think about it too long, you'll never do it. All you can think about are the things that can go wrong and how bad it's going to be, but there's nothing more rewarding than having your own business. It's second only to having your own child."

Pamela certainly wasn't born with a silver spoon in her mouth. She survived the repossession of her car, her house, hospitalization with a severe back injury, and desertion by her husband. A second back injury caused by a drunken driver forced her to work at home, for she was able to move out of bed for only one hour each day. So with the help of two co-workers and loans from friends and relatives, she started her consulting business that became so successful. And her office is still in her home so she can keep her eye on her teenagers!

Now let me help you determine your own entrepreneurial qualities and capabilities. Amazingly, most successful entrepreneurs were *not* high achievers in school and they were not active in school activities. They often preferred to be alone. Those who started childhood moneymaking projects, such as a lemonade stand, are usually successful in their own businesses. Determination to do things one's own way is a hallmark of an entrepreneur. A successful entrepreneur is daring and willing to take risks. Being tired of the daily routine is another sign of a potential entrepreneur. She must be willing to use her own savings to get started and be willing to work as long as it takes to finish any job. A successful entrepreneur will be optimistic and self-confident. She will put her goals down in writing.

Finally, let me say that all you need do to become a multimil-lionaire yourself is to come up with something that people want and need that doesn't cost a lot of money and you'll have it made. A new idea, courage, and persistence are all it will take.

Instant
Solutions
to Problems
Outside the
Workplace

In Part Two I will discuss specifically the techniques you can use to solve problems and handle situations that can sometimes occur with your friends, neighbors, and social acquaintances.

Although this part deals primarily with problems outside the workplace, the principles, techniques, and methods you will learn here can also be used successfully in your daily business relationships as well.

CONNECTING WITH PEOPLE

It is quite normal to be shy and reluctant to strike up a conversation with another person, especially if that individual is a stranger. So if you feel that way, don't feel you'll never be a success. You are not alone. In fact, you're in good company. Even seasoned actors and actresses will tell you that they get butterflies in the stomach before appearing in front of an audience—so do professional speakers.

For instance, Gert Behenna, an extremely popular author and lecturer, says that she suffered untold agonies before every one of her talks. But gradually, her fear lessened as she kept on speaking— until she finally completely overcame it, simply by repeatedly doing the thing she was afraid to do.

So you see, to overcome your shyness in talking with people, you, too, must do the thing you fear to do so you will have the power to do it. There is no other way. This concept applies to everything you do in life. If you want to become an artist, then you must paint. If you want to be a writer, then you must write. If you want to be an expert swimmer, then you must get in the water and swim. The same point can be made for golf, baseball, selling, music, and so on. You must make the first move yourself. No one else can do that for you. Until you do that, you'll never gain the power to do anything—and that includes overcoming your shyness in talking with people, even doing such a simple thing as speaking your mind in your Sunday School Class.

Project your individuality at a social function.

Here is a technique that will not only show you how to project your own individuality at a party, but will also help you overcome your shyness in talking with people at the same time.

One of the major problems in talking with others is that people can't get beyond "How are you?" "How's the wife?" "How's business?" "Beautiful day, isn't it?" "Looks like it might rain." and the like.

If you want to get out of this conversational rut that leads nowhere, then start off with a bold opening statement. Let me give you an example of what I mean:

I watched an unmarried friend of mine, Al J., as he worked this technique to perfection the other night at a social get-together. When he was introduced to an especially attractive young woman, instead of mumbling, "Hello, how are you, it's so nice to meet you," as everyone else had done, he said, "You're really going to be a problem to me tonight!"

Startled at his remark, she replied, "Why do you say that?"

"Because you're so beautiful I'll never be able to take my eyes off you," Al said. "I hope you don't mind."

"Mind?" she asked. "Of course not. How could I mind?"

With just one little sentence, Al was off and running far ahead of the pack. Of course, if you're married, this kind of an opener might not be appropriate for you to use, especially if your spouse is present!

To best project your individuality and overcome your shyness of people, try to steer the conversation to a topic of your choosing, using a *topic-teaser*. To make sure you're on safe ground, choose a topic in which you're well versed so you won't get caught short. Avoid controversial subjects that can create enemies for you.

Abortion, for example, is hardly a subject for parties or social gatherings. No matter which side you choose, you'll be in trouble. If you're for abortion, some will view you as a person who advocates murder. If you're against abortion, others will view you as being out of touch with reality.

Either way, you'll lose, so don't use such controversial subjects for an opener or a topic-teaser. You might do as I have done on those occasions when I've been asked my views on abortion. To avoid controversy and an argument, my answer has always been, "I don't feel I can honestly address that issue. I think you should ask that question of a woman."

Of course, you do want a subject that's interesting enough to stimulate a spirited conversation, but not one that creates enemies and hard feelings. Look through your newspaper or the latest good magazine. You'll be able to find more interesting topics to discuss than the weather, politics, or the state of your health.

SOLUTIONS: HOW TO ATTRACT ATTENTION AT SOCIAL FUNCTIONS

Time your arrival for your own benefit.

If your boss is hosting a social function for you and other employees, show up a few minutes early and offer to help. Don't get there too early or he'll still be in the bedroom dressing. I don't mean to imply that you should act as a maid or a butler, but you can offer to help him greet people at the door. That makes you look as if you were the co-host and gives the impression that you and your boss are really close. Back at the office, people will view you with a great deal more respect.

However, if your intent is to impress the entire group with your arrival, come just a bit late—after you're sure that everyone else is there. Then make a dramatic entrance like a conquering hero returning home from the wars. This technique will work for you only if it's a routine party given just for the sake of socializing. It will not work if the party is being given for some VIP. In that case, it's best to arrive a few minutes early and offer your services as I've mentioned.

Make a dramatic entrance that commands attention.

If you want to be the center of attention at a party or a social event, you must *dare to be different.* I don't mean that you should be so different as to cause people to laugh at you; for example, wearing jeans to a formal dinner. (To get away with that, you have to be so important and famous that you don't need to attract attention from anyone at all.) But if you dress like everyone else, look like everyone else, and act like everyone else, you'll never stand out from the crowd. Let me give you an example of how to be different and command attention without being obnoxious about it.

Elmer Leterman was one of the most ingenious and successful life insurance salesmen this country has ever known. He was well known for his style and taste in clothes. Elmer was constantly experimenting with new ideas without overstepping the boundaries of good taste.

For instance, at a particular awards dinner attended by the top business leaders of the entire country, everyone was dressed in formal midnight blue tuxedos with starched white shirts. That is, everyone except Elmer Leterman. When he made his dramatic entrance, all eyes in the ballroom turned to look at him, for he was dressed in a magnificent gray silk formal tuxedo with black satin trim. Although properly dressed and in perfectly good taste, Elmer was the center of attention simply because he had the courage to be different.

Other ways to gain attention.

Some years ago, I met Gary Davis, a young up-and-coming insurance salesman in his company's regional office in Orlando, Florida.

Gary was only five feet four inches tall. He was a quite common, ordinary-looking person except for one thing. He wore a fiery red beard, and this was long before beards were commonplace. "Why the beard?" I asked him.

"To attract attention," Gary said. "I want to make sure people notice me and remember me. You wear your mustache for the same reason, don't you?"

I had to admit he was right. People remember me as "that man with the salt-and-pepper (now mostly salt!) mustache." If it were not for that, perhaps many of them wouldn't remember the slightly overweight, rather short older man with thinning hair who wears glasses. Unfortunately, that description fits most American men over fifty. But people do remember that fellow with the "distinguished-looking mustache."

Incidentally, that young insurance salesman is now a division manager and the assistant vice president of his company. Somebody topside kept him in mind. And he still sports that flaming red beard, too.

My point is that you need to be distinctive in some way to be noticed and remembered. Whatever your most striking attribute happens to be, develop it to the fullest. Some famous people used a physical feature that might be considered a detriment to attract attention. For instance, what would Jimmy Durante have been without his big nose, Eddie Cantor without his pop eyes, Joe E. Brown without his huge mouth, or Marlene Dietrich without her beautiful legs?

One of the best physical attributes you can develop to attract attention is your voice. Your style of talking and the way you converse with others can make a vital contribution to your reputation and your success.

I am fortunate in having a deep, resonant baritone voice that people remember well. Two years ago, I saw a lady whom I'd met for just a few brief hours nearly forty years before. "I wouldn't have remembered your face, for you didn't have a mustache then," she said. "But the moment you spoke, I recognized you. Your voice is so distinctive that no one could possibly forget it."

Still more ways to command attention.

Always keep in mind that *color and movement* are two important ways to attract attention and hold it. For example, if you can do any magic tricks, use those two principles of color and movement to attract and hold everyone's attention. You don't have to make rabbits or doves appear and disappear from your hat or saw a woman in half. I remember a sergeant I met in the army who was an amateur magician. He entertained at both NCO clubs and officers' clubs and made a small fortune.

His two major feats of legerdemain were done with ping-pong balls and cards. People were absolutely fascinated by his tricks with ping-pong balls. He would make them appear and disappear from his mouth, his ear, his nose, behind the back of his hand, and so on.

I watched him dozens of times put six or eight ping-pong balls in his mouth one at a time and then open his mouth to show that they were no longer there. He also had a variety of card tricks that kept his audience baffled and spellbound.

I used to be able to snap quarters up my coat sleeve with my fingers and then pull them out from behind a person's ear until arthritis caught up with me and my fingers got too stiff. You lose your audience in a hurry when the quarters fall on the floor!

My father-in-law had a clever trick in which a marked dime that he put in his pocket ended up inside a tiny cloth sack inside a small matchbox that was wrapped with several rubber bands.

Simple card tricks that are easy to do can still attract and baffle an audience. Not only can you gain and hold people's attention, but you can also have a lot of fun at the same time. And if you get good enough with your magic tricks, you'll find that you'll have more party invitations than you can handle.

SOLUTIONS: HOW TO MAKE SURE YOU'LL NEVER BE INVITED ANYWHERE

I attended a small social gathering one afternoon at a friend's house. One of the people present was a talkative man who constantly forced his opinions on everyone. Whatever subject was brought up, he'd either done it before or knew all about it. He was an expert on everything, at least according to his account of it.

"Good heavens, is there anything that man doesn't know?" Jack J. asked me.

"Evidently not, Jack," I replied. "But I doubt if he'll ever be invited here again."

If you don't want to be a loner and not be invited anywhere, then don't be a *know-it-all*. A know-it-all rubs people the wrong way. This kind of person embarrasses others, makes everyone uncomfortable, and is highly unpopular. Nobody likes the perfect person who has all the answers to everything.

I don't mean you must always run yourself down or be considered ignorant to be popular and well liked. But it is utterly refreshing to hear a person say, "I don't know."

When I was in the service I spent a great deal of time teaching classes in tactics. If I was asked a question to which I did not know the answer, I didn't try to pretend or bluff my way through. Instead, I always said, "I don't know, but if it's important to you, I'll find out and let you know."

I don't know are three magic words you can use to great advantage. If you don't know and the other person does know, he'll be sure to tell you. And even if you do know the subject, so what? Your aim is to be well liked and popular with others, not to show off your knowledge. You'll never achieve your goal if you're always going to be a know-it-all.

So even if you do know the answers when someone is trying to introduce an interesting subject, just be tactful and diplomatic enough to say "I don't know" and give the other person a chance to shine.

Another sure-fire way to be a loner and never be invited anywhere is to constantly interrupt others and force your opinions on them. When you do this, you're trampling on the person's ego, his desire to be important, to be heard and to be recognized. By interrupting others you'll not only be unpopular, you'll also be disliked.

I know of no quicker way to insult a person or to hurt her feelings than to interrupt her when she's trying to tell you something. How many times have you been right in the middle of a good story only to have one of your listeners interrupt you and start talking on a brand-new subject? You'd have liked to strangle her with your bare hands, right?

I know exactly how you feel, for one of my close friends did this to me once in front of a large group of people and embarrassed me greatly. It took me longer than I care to admit to get over my resentment toward him for what he'd done to me.

SOLUTIONS: HOW TO WIN LASTING FRIENDS

First, let me give you a seventeen-point checklist you can use to win friends. Then I'll give you a list of fifteen techniques that you can use to keep those friendships warm and cordial.

WINNING FRIENDS

1. Be yourself. If you try to be someone you are not, you'll appear phony and artificial.

2. Give of yourself to the other person. Do everything in your power to increase the happiness and success of the other individual.

3. Find a common denominator on which to build a solid friendship.

4. Use praise, not flattery, to gain a person's friendship. Praise compliments a person for what he *does;* flattery for what he *is.*

5. Accept a person exactly as he or she is; never criticize an individual if you want to retain his or her friendship.

6. Listen carefully to other people's opinions.

7. Ask questions that encourage others to talk.

8. Offer opinions rather than irrefutable facts.

9. Maintain a sense of humor; don't take yourself too seriously.

10. Accept correction gracefully for your mistakes.

11. Be cheerful, friendly, and optimistic. Smile.

12. Avoid arguments and disagreements at all costs. They gain you no benefit whatever, but they can generate a great amount of ill will. Give ground on unimportant trifles.

13. Don't gossip or be a rumormonger.

14. Talk about subjects the other person is interested in.

15. Don't be a know-it-all or a perfectionist.

16. Don't set up your own standards of right and wrong.

17. Learn how to mix business and friendship successfully.

Keeping friends.

Once you've made those friends, it takes a lot of effort to keep your friendships warm and cordial. Neglect them and they'll die from lack of care. You can use this list of fifteen techniques to keep your friendships alive and well:

1. Always maintain a warm, friendly attitude toward others.

2. Go out of your way to perform some unexpected service for your friends, or better yet, for your enemies.

3. Compliment another person and praise him for something that he has done.

4. Always keep your word. Never make a promise you cannot keep or a decision you cannot support.

5. Treat your associates at work as close friends of long standing, not just casual acquaintances.

6. Establish a reputation as a reliable person who can be depended on, so your friends will trust you.

7. Go to work with a smile on your face, leaving your personal problems and troubles at home.

8. Never use your position for personal gain at someone else's expense.

9. Don't play favorites; treat everyone equally.

10. Have respect for every person's dignity. Treat every woman like a lady and every man like a gentleman.

11. Be sincere in your relationships with others. Don't be a phony. Really mean what you say and say what you mean.

12. Practice the Golden Rule with everyone, especially your associates.

13. Maintain a strong belief in the rights of others.

14. Have an abiding interest in the other person's welfare.

15. Be willing to deal with every person as courteously and considerately as if he or she were a relative.

SOLUTIONS: HOW TO MIX FRIENDSHIP AND BUSINESS SUCCESSFULLY

Any person who says you cannot mix friendship and business doesn't know much about business. Would you do business with a person you didn't like? Of course not. Neither would I. In fact, I don't. Let me explain that more fully to you:

As I said before, about two blocks from where I live there is a large supermarket. But I never shop there, for the clerks are surly, sour-faced, and ill-mannered. Instead, I drive two miles to a supermarket where the clerks are all friendly, greet you with a big smile, and say "thank you" to your face instead of staring at the cash register.

Friendship is the best sales technique of all, no matter what business you're in or what your job happens to be. Friendship is responsible for more good human relations in business, for meeting more sales quotas and building more big bank accounts than anything else.

Let me give you another example of a very successful corporation president and chief executive officer I know who has an open-door policy. In fact, there isn't a door on his office at all, for he's had it completely removed so all his employees can have easy access to him.

He is on friendly terms with every single person in his whole company and it's a big one. He has never become snobbish or high hat about his position or his success.

He insists on being called by his nickname, "Doug," and will not answer to "Mr. Douglas" or "Mr. President." Whenever a person calls him "Mr. Douglas," he looks at him and says, "Who?" If the person calls him Mr. Douglas again, he continues to look at the individual and again says, "Who?" He will not talk to the person, whether the person is a janitor, an executive, a production-line employee, or a manager, until the person finally calls him "Doug."

Although there is an executive restaurant for top brass, he always eats in the employee cafeteria and shoots the breeze during the lunch hour.

He still approaches his people with comments like these:

1. Do you think this procedure would be a better one?

2. Thanks for doing such a terrific job on this for me.

3. I'm sure you understand this, but I can't figure it out. Would you please explain it to me?

4. I've always admired your good judgment in matters like this.

5. I'm sure you could solve this problem in no time at all for me.

6. What is your own opinion on this? I'd like to know what you think about it before I make up my mind.

7. What's your solution to this problem? I know you're an expert in this field.

8. Could you help me out of this mess?

As you can see, these comments appeal to a person's ego and make him or her feel important. As you could easily guess, every employee in the plant goes all out and does his level best for "Doug."

MAKING FRIENDS, NOT ENEMIES

SOLUTIONS: HOW TO AVOID MAKING ENEMIES

In order to show you how to keep from making enemies, I want to tell you about a few bad moves that are guaranteed to create enemies for you. Avoid them at all costs. You'll be much better off when you do.

1. *Malicious gossip and slander create enemies*. An old adage goes like this: "If you can't say anything good about someone, then don't say anything at all." I have never been able to understand why some individuals take such a perverse delight in slandering other people.

Maybe when they see that another person is in some sort of trouble, they are so happy it didn't happen to them that they can't keep from talking about it. Unfortunately, they magnify and amplify the incident until the facts are so distorted that the end result is slander and malicious gossip. Let me tell you about something that happened to a friend of mine.

"Some years ago our youngest son was visiting us and became very ill," Norman told me. "He was so sick, he was carried into the hospital's emergency room in a near coma. He was severely dehy-drated and barely conscious. For three days he was in intensive care. Finally, after ten days of lab analysis, consultations, and so on, a final diagnosis was made: He had a severe case of juvenile diabetes.

"Now at the time our son was wearing his hair down to his shoulders, and although I didn't care for his long hairstyle, I had said nothing. After all, it was his hair, not mine.

"But a particularly vicious-tongued neighbor of ours, who regarded every young person with long hair as a hippie or a freak of some sort, spread the word throughout the neighborhood that our son was a dope addict and had been taken to the hospital suffering from an overdose of drugs! After she learned that the diagnosis was diabetes, she retraced her steps, warning everyone never to repeat what she had said. But one of my oldest and closest friends told me what had happened.

"I never retaliated in any way, but needless to say, our friend-ship was reduced to that of a mere nodding acquaintance, and frankly we would cross the street to keep from meeting her.

"I later learned that this woman and her husband had moved from three previous homes simply because they had destroyed the relationship with their neighbors by slanderous gossip. I wonder how long it will be before they will be forced to move again?"

So don't gossip or maliciously slander another person. Not only will you lose your friends, but you'll also pick up a lot of enemies along the way.

2. *Telling people they're wrong is another sure way of creating enemies.* Last year, I was on the Chamber of Commerce committee that was responsible for soliciting contributions from busi-nesspeople to make up food baskets for the needy at Christmastime.

My friend Gene Baxter and I went together on most occasions, feeling that it was easier to collect with two people. One old, grumpy fellow complained loudly about giving. "I don't believe in charity," he said. "Nobody ever gave me anything. The Bible says that God helps those who help themselves."

"I agree with you," I said, "But we're not asking for much. Besides, it's the children we want to help out. After all, they're not old enough to help themselves as you so wisely suggest."

After we left with his check in hand, Gene said, "Jim, I've never heard that Bible quotation, have you?"

"No, Gene, I haven't," I said, "because it isn't in the Bible. But if we'd told him he was wrong, we wouldn't have his check, now would we?"

There's no point in telling a person he's wrong. When you do, you're criticizing him, and criticism destroys friendships. Not only that, it creates enemies. Most of us can't even stand being told that our watch is wrong, let alone being criticized for something more important.

Now if you're a boss or if you're planning on becoming one some day, I know there'll be times when you need to correct another person's mistakes. But remember to correct the mistake; don't criticize the person while you're doing it.

3. *Ridicule someone and you'll create an enemy for life*. When you ridicule someone, you deflate his ego and destroy his feeling of pride and importance. Ridicule maims and cripples people psychologically, often permanently.

You see, a person will tolerate almost any insult, defeat, or injury and accept it with some semblance of good grace. He'll probably tolerate a great deal of abuse from you and still treat you like a civilized human being.

But if you make fun of a person, if you belittle and ridicule him, or if you make a fool of him—especially in front of others—you'll have made an enemy for the rest of your life. Not only have you deflated his ego and injured his pride, but you've also attacked his sense of self-respect, dignity, and self-esteem.

So if you do ridicule someone and make fun of him, better bolt the doors and bar the windows, for he'll come after you—and that's for sure.

The basic desire for revenge, vengeance, an eye for an eye and a tooth for a tooth can be a greater driving force than even the desire for importance or the desire for sexual gratification.

Now let's find out *How to Turn an Enemy into a True Friend*.

SOLUTIONS: HOW TO TURN AN ENEMY INTO A TRUE FRIEND

When you convert your enemies into friends, you'll win these three big benefits:

1. *You'll gain many, many true friends,* for if you're like most of us, you'll start out with lots of enemies to convert.

2. *Former enemies will learn to admire and respect you* when you turn them into friends instead.

3. *You'll establish your reputation as an expert in the art of human relations,* for converting enemies into friends requires tact, diplomacy, and skill.

For starters, if you want to make a friend out of an enemy, it's up to you to make the first move. Otherwise, it isn't going to happen. Here's an example of how you can take that first step:

Once upon a time, there lived in the small town of Suburbia two neighbors named George and Jim. But they were not good neighbors. They just lived next to each other. They had long been at odds, although neither could remember exactly why. They just knew they didn't like each other and that was reason enough as far as they were concerned.

So they lived in a constant state of bitter verbal warfare. Most of the time they would not even speak at all, although in the summertime their lawnmowers often rubbed wheels as they moved along their backyard battle lines.

Then, late one summer, George and his wife went on a two-week vacation. At first, Jim and his wife didn't even notice that they were gone. After all, why should they? They seldom spoke to each other, anyway, unless one of them had a specific complaint to register with the other.

But one evening, just after he'd finished mowing his yard, Jim noticed how high George's grass had become. It was especially obvious now that he'd just mowed his own lawn.

Anyone driving by would recognize that George and his wife were not at home and had not been there for quite some time, Jim thought. In fact, it was an open invitation for a burglar to break in, Jim mused to himself. And then like lightning, a sudden flash of inspiration hit him. *Don't try to love your neighbor—just help him.*

"I looked at that high grass again and my mind rebelled at the thought of helping someone I so thoroughly disliked," Jim says. "But in spite of all my efforts to blot the idea out of my mind, it persisted. It just wouldn't go away. So the next morning I mowed his blasted lawn!

"A few days later, on a Sunday afternoon, George and Dora came home. Shortly after they got back, I saw him walking up and down the street. He was stopping at every house in the block.

"At last he knocked on my door. When I opened it, he just stood there staring at me, an odd and puzzled expression wrinkling up his face.

"After what seemed like an eternity to me, he spoke. 'Jim, did you mow my lawn?' he finally asked. It was the first time he'd called me by my first name in a long while. 'I've asked everyone else on the block. No one else mowed it. Jack said you did it. Is that true, did you mow my lawn?' His tone was almost accusatory as if I'd committed some crime.

"'Yes, George, I did,' I said, almost belligerently, for I was waiting for him to blow his stack at me for going on his property.

"He hesitated for a moment, as if searching for the right thing to say. Finally he muttered in a low, almost inaudible voice, 'Thanks,' and then he turned sharply and walked quickly away."

And so the ice had finally been broken for George and Jim. Oh, they're not playing golf or bowling together yet, and their wives don't run back and forth every day to borrow sugar or salt or chitchat. But they are making progress. At least they are smiling at each other as their lawnmowers pass in the backyard. They even say "Hi!" once in a while. They seem to have declared a truce of sorts, and their former backyard battleground is now a demilitarized zone. And who knows? They might even share a cup of coffee together one of these days.

Turn an enemy into a friend with love? Perhaps, but only if you spell the word *love* H-E-L-P! How can I be so sure of that? Oh, that's easy. You see, I'm Jim.

SOLUTIONS: HOW TO TURN OFF A PERSON'S ANGER IMMEDIATELY

There can be many different reasons for a person to be angry with you or to view you with suspicion and mistrust. It could be because of something you've said or done. It might be because of something he *thinks* you've said or done.

Sometimes, a person will take her anger at something else—for instance, the company or corporation, the government, society as a whole—out on you, only because you happen to be the closest or most convenient target. Finally, some people's imaginations work overtime. They have the idea that everybody in the whole world is against them or out to get them.

But no matter what the cause of a person's anger, you'll want to turn it off immediately so you can restore normal relations with him or her again. You can do that easily if you will use the techniques I'll give you in this chapter.

Calming down an angry neighbor.

When your neighbor gets angry with you for some reason or other, you can do one of two things: You can get mad and fight back or you can take steps to defuse his anger.

Now if you fight back and retaliate—which is precisely what the other person expects you to do—you will lose complete control of the situation and only make things worse. You will accomplish absolutely nothing if you lose your temper, too. In fact, the inability to control one's temper indicates a definite lack of self-discipline.

What happens, then, if you don't fight back? Does this mean that the other individual will automatically win? Of course not. The only time you can be sure of winning is when you don't lose your temper and retaliate. It takes at least two people to make a fight. When you refuse to become angry, the other person's anger will burn itself out. Let me give you an example:

"I have a next-door neighbor with a short fuse who flies off the handle for almost any reason," Kenneth N. told me. "It used to be that when he came over raising the devil about something, I'd get mad, yell back, and we'd get nowhere. We always ended up with a shouting match until I learned how to handle his anger.

"Now when he gets mad at me—which seldom happens anymore since he knows he can't win—I simply remain calm and quiet instead of flying off the handle, too. When I refuse to fight, he realizes he might as well cuss out a tree or a bush, so he throws in the towel and gives up."

The best way to turn off your neighbor's anger immediately is to respond in a kind and friendly manner. Remain completely calm.

Say nothing until he has drained himself emotionally. Then answer him quietly and softly, for as the Bible says, "A soft answer turneth away wrath," and that's so true. If you use a quiet, soft tone of voice, it will not only calm the other person down, but it will also keep you from getting angry as well.

When you refuse to fight back, when you hold your temper in check and speak softly, the angry person soon realizes that he's the only one yelling. This embarrasses him and makes him feel like a fool. He will suddenly become extremely self-conscious and anxious to get the situation back to normal as soon as possible.

You can use this applied psychology technique to control an angry person's emotions until she becomes rational and reasonable again. So when you find yourself in a tense situation with an angry person, stay cool and calm. Deliberately lower your voice and keep it down. This will motivate the angry individual to lower her voice. As long as you speak softly, she cannot possibly remain angry and highstrung for very long.

Using the "fact-finder" technique.

No matter what the cause of a person's anger, and no matter who the individual is, it's up to you to find out what the problem is so you can correct it and restore friendly relations.

The best way to do this is to use the "fact-finder" technique. In other words, play detective and go after all the facts. Ask questions of *what, who, when, where, why,* and *how* until you discover why he's angry.

Find out *why* the person is angry, *what* made him mad, *who* made him angry, *when* did it happen, *where, how?* Ask *what* you can do to set things right after you find out what's wrong.

I always use the fact-finder technique to find the reason behind a person's anger. Even when I think I have all the answers, I will ask one more question: "Is there any other reason for you to be upset about this?" Here's an example of how well this method works.

Sam Pierce, a young salesman for a vitamin products company, attended one of my business seminars. He told me about a big account with a large health clinic that his company had lost and was not able to regain. I suggested he go back to call on them again and use the fact-finder technique to find out what had gone wrong. A month later, I received this letter from him:

"As you suggested, I went back and requested an interview with the chief administrative officer of the clinic. Our conversation went like this:

"'Dr. Smith, my company would like to know exactly *why* we lost your business. You must have had a good reason for leaving us for no one makes a better product more economically than we do. If we were guilty of some mistake, we'd like to know what it is so we won't make the same mistake with someone else. Will you please tell me what we did wrong?'

"After a long silence, he said, 'Your company president promised me an extra five percent discount because of our large volume of purchases. But when I received your bill, it was for the full amount. There was no extra discount. I had my controller call your accounting department to find out why. They told her the company never gave extra discounts to anyone, no matter how much they purchased. I figured I'd been lied to just to get our business, so I quit your company and went somewhere else.'

"I knew there had to be a mistake somewhere, so I asked Dr. Smith if I could call my office collect right then and find out where the error was. When I talked to the company president, the mistake was discovered immediately. He had simply forgotten to tell our accounting department about the special five percent discount for Dr. Smith's health clinic.

"I asked him to speak with Dr. Smith right then and there so this misunderstanding could be cleared up. The president apologized for his mistake and assured Dr. Smith that he would receive the extra discount on all past orders that had already been delivered as well as on future orders. As a result, we regained the biggest account our company has, all because I used your fact-finder technique and refused to give up until I had all the answers."

Turn off a person's anger with an apology.

To say you're sorry, even when you're wrong, seems to come hard to most people. It's difficult to apologize. But when you're wrong, you ought to quickly admit it. I know of no faster or better way to turn off a person's anger than to apologize to the individual whose feelings you've hurt.

I once had occasion to write to a lawyer with whom I was extremely unhappy. I felt the fee he'd charged me was far too high, and I told him so. I guess I got carried away, for my letter became more caustic than I'd meant it to be.

He called me to tell me in no uncertain terms what he thought of both me and my letter. He was really angry and he laid it on hot and heavy. When he finally paused for breath, I cut in and said "Brad, I'm truly sorry I wrote that letter in such haste. I should never have done so. I apologize for what I said. You have a perfect right to be upset. Please forgive me."

He was quiet for several long moments and then he said, "That's okay, Jim. I admire you for having the courage to say you were wrong and apologize. Perhaps my fee was a bit too high, so I guess I owe you an apology, too. I'll send you a new one. Let's start all over so we can be friends again, okay?"

So you see, to promptly admit your mistake when you're wrong and apologize to the person you've hurt can immediately clear the air and turn his anger into friendship. But you can go even further than that for even better results.

Say you're sorry even when you're not at fault.

When you're not in the wrong, you can afford to be big about things. If just saying you're sorry will restore peace in the family or friendly relations between two people, then say it so you can get on with the more important business of enjoying each other's companionship, rather than fretting and stewing about who's right or who's wrong.

SOLUTIONS: A SIX-STEP TECHNIQUE FOR WINNING ARGUMENTS

Almost every day, some circumstance will come up where you need to get another person to accept your viewpoint or to see things your way. Whether or not you accomplish that depends primarily on how you try to win the argument.

The method that most people use to try to win an argument is force. If you use force in an attempt to overpower or intimidate your opponent, your argument will turn into nothing more than a shouting match and an ego battle.

But this is a complete waste of time. You cannot win an argument by forcefully ramming your ideas down the other person's throat. The only way you can ever really win an argument is to get the other person to change his mind.

To win an argument, you must work *with* human nature, not *against* it. If you want a person to see things your way, don't force your ideas on him. Your ideas must become *his* ideas before he will ever accept them. When he has convinced himself that your viewpoint is correct, he will change his mind voluntarily. When he sees things your way, when he makes your viewpoint his viewpoint, you'll win your argument; but not until that happens.

You can get a person to accept your idea only when you appeal to his emotions as well as to his reason, logic, and common sense. As I mentioned previously, the head never hears 'til the heart has listened, but that's such an important concept it's worth repeating several times. You cannot possibly win an argument until that happens. Here, now, are six guidelines you can use to win an argument every single time.

1. ***Retain control of the argument at all times***. Don't jump the gun and try to win by stating your side of the case first. If you do, you'll reveal your position and expose your vulnerable points. When you try to get your licks in first, you allow the initiative to pass to your opponent. You must retain control of the situation yourself.

Although it might sound paradoxical, the best way to do this is to let the other person state his argument first. Don't interrupt. Let him talk himself out so he will exhaust himself.

It is an extremely good idea to get the person to repeat some of his key points or his sore spots. Letting him get it all off his chest helps immeasurably. If you can get him to repeat his complaints several times, he literally drains himself mentally. That makes it much easier for you to win when he's emotionally fatigued and worn out.

2. ***Probe and explore his argument***. Unless the person is ready to receive a particular idea, he is not likely to accept it. Lead him on an objective fact-finding survey of his position until you find a weakness in his argument.

When you find such a weakness, use it for your opening statement to persuade him of your viewpoint. When he sees that weakness for himself, he will become much more receptive to your ideas.

That's why you should always let him talk first. You get his ideas out into the open, where you can probe them for weaknesses. The moment he realizes there are some holes in his argument, the more willing he will be to accept your point of view.

3. *Know when to take action.* There's no point in attempting any action until you know the person is receptive to change. Listen for comments like these: "I could be wrong on a point or two, I'm willing to listen to reason, I've never looked at it that way before, I could be mistaken on this one small detail."

When you hear expressions of self-doubt like these, it's a clear signal to you that it's time to take action and present your side of the case.

4. *State your side of the argument.* The tendency is always to use the old forceful methods to win an argument. Using force seems to be built right into us. But you must discipline yourself to avoid this bad habit of trying to show the other fellow up. Even if you outtalk him to the point where he can say nothing in rebuttal, *you still will not win until he accepts your viewpoint as his own.*

It's a proven fact that the best way to state your case is to do so moderately, accurately, and with sincerity. Be enthusiastic but don't let your enthusiasm carry you away emotionally so that you exaggerate or approach too forcefully.

5. *Don't be greedy.* Most people who use force to argue try to prove the other person completely wrong on *every* single point. They insist on winning 100 percent. This is a mistake. A skillful person who uses persuasion rather than force to win an argument will always be willing to concede something to his opponent or to give ground on some minor matter.

So be flexible. Compromise a bit; bend with the wind. Politicians do that to survive. The smart ones live on; the stubborn ones do not. So give in here and there on small points. Just follow this next rule and you will always be safe: Give ground on trifles—never on principles. But learn to tell the difference between the two.

6. ***Help the person save face***. Not being greedy or not insisting on winning your case 100 percent helps the other person save face. But you can do much more than that. Here's how:

Many times your opponent realizes he's wrong. He's already changed his mind and wants to agree with you, but his ego gets in the way of his good judgment; his pride keeps him from admitting his mistake. If you find your opponent in that spot, open the door for him. Help him find a way out of his dilemma.

One way you can do this is to suggest that he might not have had all the facts when he made up his mind. You might say something like this, "John, if you didn't know about this, I can see why you made the decision you did. I'd have done the same thing."

Even if John did have all the facts, he'll grab at this lifeline you've just thrown him. All he needs to do is say he didn't have that fact and he's out of his corner. You've achieved your goal. You've helped him save face.

DEALING WITH STRANGERS

SOLUTIONS: HOW TO STRIKE UP A CONVERSATION WITH A STRANGER

Before I tell you how to strike up a conversation with a complete stranger, I want to tell you what not to do: *Never open a conversation by just saying "Hello."* It's a deadly opening because it's not interesting, so the conversation goes nowhere.

The magic key to a successful opening is to get the other person's interest immediately if you want your conversation or your talk to be successful and beneficial. Now for the techniques you can use to do exactly that:

One of the best ways you can strike up a conversation with a stranger and make him feel completely at ease talking with you is to pay him some sort of a compliment, appeal to his ego, make him feel important. Do that and you'll have him eating out of your hand in no time at all. Here are some examples of how to use that technique:

1. "I've always been interested in computers, but I really don't understand how they work. I know you're an expert in that field. Could you tell me more about them?" (This opening can be used for any kind of profession or occupation.)

2. "I've often wished I knew more about the stock market and how it works. Would you tell me more about your position as a stockbroker and the kind of work you do?" (This opening can also be used for any occupation or profession.)

3. "I've never seen such good-looking shoes before. Could you tell me what kind of leather they're made of?"

4. "I've never met an educator I didn't enjoy talking with for I always learn something new. Could you tell me more about your particular specialty?"

5. "You really have a gorgeous tan. I'd love to look like that, but I always turn as red as a boiled lobster. What's your secret?"

Although you can use other conversation starters, I've found that using a leading question to get the person to talk about herself and her own interests is the most reliable way to get a stranger to open up and talk with you.

If you know nothing at all about the other person's background, you can always compliment a man on his jacket, his shoes, his wavy hair, whatever is striking about him. If the individual is a woman, you can compliment her on her choice of jewelry, her clothing, her hairdo, her beauty.

It doesn't matter how you do it or what you say as long as you feed the other person's ego. Make him or her feel important and you'll never go wrong. It's one of the best ways in the world to strike up a conversation with a stranger. You'll always be remembered as a most interesting person who was a brilliant and scintillating conversationalist, even if you hardly say a word.

SOLUTIONS: HOW TO GET A TOTAL STRANGER TO HELP YOU

If you want to get a person you've never met before to do something, then say something that will let the other person know immediately that he is superior to you in some way.

The plain truth is that every person you meet feels he is better than you in one way or another. A sure way to his heart is for you to let him know that you recognize his superiority. All you need do is ask a person for his advice, his opinion, or his help, and he'll go out of his way to help you.

I can recall when I first became interested in bowling. Naturally, I didn't know how or where to begin. I was looking at bowling balls, shoes, wrist supports, and so on. The bowling alley manager was all tied up with the details of a league so he couldn't help me out for the moment.

I lifted one ball after another off the rack by the counter only to put it back. Then I noticed a woman on my left smiling and watching me sympathetically.

"Can you help me out?" I asked. "I've never bowled before and I just don't know where to start."

"Sure, let me give you a hand," she said. "I'll be glad to show you the tricks of the trade and help you get started."

That lady spent the entire afternoon helping me select the right ball and shoes and teaching me the rudiments of bowling.

If you'll just be willing to admit that some person could be superior to you in some way and then ask for help, you'll soon find that a tremendous number of benefits will come your way.

Here are some specific phrases you can use to get the benefit you want:

1. Can you help me out with this, please?

2. Could I ask for your advice?

3. What is your opinion on this?

4. I value your judgment on this matter.

5. Could you please show me how to do this?

6. I would much appreciate your telling me how to do this.

7. I know you're an expert in this field. Could you give me a few tips on how to handle it?

These phrases and others like them will help you ask for help from a complete stranger and feel completely at ease about it.

I do know this. *Every person I meet is my superior in one way or another and in that I learn from him or her.* If you will just remember this idea, you'll have no trouble in putting this technique to work so you can gain the benefits for yourself.

SOLUTIONS: THREE WAYS TO FORM A FRIENDSHIP RIGHT AWAY

It's easy to strike up a conversation with someone you don't know and form a friendship if you just get your mind off yourself and what you want and concentrate on what the other person is interested in.

There are any number of conversation openers you can use to control the situation and get the other person to talk, but the three most effective, in the order of their importance, are a person's name, vocation, and hobby. Here's what I mean:

1. **Ask about the person's name.** A person's name is the most important word in all the world to him, so all you need say is something like this:

"Your name is fascinating. I don't think I've ever heard it before. Would you tell me more about its ethnic origin and its meaning?" Let me give you an example of this technique.

When I first met John Fowler, I said that to him. I was amazed when he glared at me and said, "Well, I suppose you think I'm English. Everyone else does. But I'm not English. My ancestors came from Ireland and I dislike having people think my ancestors were English. They're not. They're Irish and I'm darned proud of that!"

"No, John, I didn't think you were English," I said. "It's just that I've never heard the name 'Fowler' before and I was interested in knowing its origin and background, for the ethnic derivation of names has always been a hobby of mine."

John relaxed then and told me about his father and mother coming to the United States, penniless and knowing no one, as a result of the failure of the potato crop and the famine that followed in the mid-1800s in Ireland.

He talked for more than an hour about his family's origins, his parents' native country, his children and grandchildren, his hobbies and interests. And as a result of my interest in names, I made a new friend that day.

I'm just as touchy about my name as John Fowler is about his. Mine is of Dutch origin. My grandparents came to this country from Rotterdam, Holland, in 1870. All my ancestors are Holland Dutch, not German, and I don't want to be thought of as German just as John Fowler didn't want to be thought of as English. We may all be United States citizens, but we still have a feeling of original ethnic pride about our names.

2. ***Every person likes to tell you what he does for a living.*** All you need say is, "I've always been interested in your profession. Would you tell me something about your position and the work that you do?"

This is usually enough to keep the other person going for half an hour or more. In fact, you might end up feeling swamped with information, as I did when I asked a young computer programmer to explain her work to me. She told me so much about computers, I thought I was going to drown in technical terms. I felt like my father did when he used to say that the preacher told him more than he wanted to know. If this happens to you, just be patient. Remember, your purpose is to control the situation and guide the conversation for your own *eventual* benefit.

3. ***Ask a person to tell you about his hobby.*** Most people have an avocation of some sort—hunting, fishing, bowling, golf, gardening, music, whatever. In a great many cases, people are as expert, if not more so, in their avocations as they are in their professions, and they always like to talk about their hobbies.

I have a neighbor who is a pharmacist by profession and a botanist by avocation. Bill is a walking encyclopedia. He can give a person valuable free advice about plants, shrubs, trees, vines, and everything else that grows. Bill can look at a plant or a shrub and tell you if it needs iron, magnesium, has too much water, not enough water, whatever. All you need to do to become his A-number-one friend is to ask him something about his hobby.

SOLUTIONS: HOW TO TALK TO THE OPPOSITE SEX

Some men find it extremely difficult to talk to a woman. They are overly worried about saying the wrong thing and having it misinterpreted as either a chauvinistic remark or a pass. Married men are often uncomfortable talking to a single woman, especially if their wives are present.

This will present no problem to you at all if you stay on safe
ground by selecting an appropriate and suitable subject. Stay away
from controversial subjects, such as abortion, for example.

Surveys of over 1,000 women about their favorite topics
for discussion revealed that the following subjects were at the
top:

1. Family and home (including children and grandchildren)

2. Good health

3. Work or job (if a working woman)

4. Promotion and advancement (if employed)

5. Personal growth

6. Clothes and shopping

7. Recreation

8. Travel

9. Men (especially single women)

Subjects that were least liked by women were sports, politics,
and religion.

I would also like to pass on this advice: If you are concerned
about having what you say interpreted as a pass or a chauvinistic
remark, just treat every woman like a lady and you'll have no trouble at all with having what you say misinterpreted.

Now let me tell you how to talk with men if you're a woman.
The topics men most like to talk about are strikingly similar to those
women like, according to surveys of 1,000 men. They like to talk
about the following subjects:

1. Family and home (including children and grandchildren)

2. Good health

3. Work or job

4. Promotion and advancement

5. Personal growth

6. Recreation

7. Travel

8. The opposite sex (especially young single men)

The men surveyed also enjoyed talking about sports and politics. They disliked discussions of religion, clothes, fashions, or shopping.

Instant Solutions to Family Problems

Some people work overtime to get along with everyone outside the home—their friends, neighbors, co-workers, business associates, boss, church members, and so on—but they do absolutely nothing to create a happy and joyous atmosphere in their own home.

For instance, a great many husbands and fathers try to control their wives and children by being the boss in the house. That sort of attitude and action on a father's part will cause children to become rebellious and leave home as soon as possible to get out from under the tyrant's iron hand. It will also quickly drive a wife to the divorce court.

Part Three, then, will give you the techniques you can use to make marriage and home life happier. When you use them, you'll enjoy a peaceful, pleasant atmosphere in your home.

CREATING A HAPPIER HOME LIFE

I can best help you understand how to use participatory management in your home by explaining how it is used in both business and industry. For example, if you're the boss and you need your subordinates to help you get the job done, you can usually get things done in one of three ways:

1. *You can give a person a direct order to do something.* Even if that person is your employee and has no other choice than to obey you, this is normally the least desirable of the three major techniques available to you, for you will usually get only the minimum effort and results.

2. *You can ask a person to help you do the work, using already established procedures.* This is better than the first method, but it still leaves a great deal to be desired. This technique is commonly called "cooperation," but that word can be highly misleading. For instance, management always says it cooperates with

labor. What this usually means is that management furnishes the methods while labor supplies the muscles. But that's not real cooperation at all; that's only giving lip service to the idea.

   3. **You can ask people for their ideas on the best way to get the job done.** This is by far the most desirable method to use. It is called *participatory management*. When you use it, you'll gain people's cooperation and full support, whether it's outside your home with your employees or inside your home with your spouse and children.

   Let me tell you why participatory management is so effective. When you ask people for their opinions and ideas on how to get the job done, you've made them feel important, and that's one of the secret motivators that turn people on.

   Making people feel important is a powerful stimulant and incentive to productivity. As a friend of mine, Dick C., told me, "I was so flattered by having the company president ask for my opinion, I couldn't get my hat on my head for more than a week!"

   Can you imagine how important you can make your son or your daughter feel when you ask them for their advice about how to cut down on utility bills, reduce the grocery bills, save money on clothing, or whatever else it might be?

   Or if you're redecorating their bedrooms, don't arbitrarily make the color selections. Allow them to voice their own opinions and their own preferences. If possible, let them make the final decisions. You might not like their choices, but after all, it is their bedrooms.

   What happens when you buy a new car? Does your spouse get a chance to help you make the decision? How about your children? Do you also get their opinions? I once bought a convertible because our three children wanted one. It was against my better judgment, for I've never been convinced that a convertible is a safe car to be in if it rolls over. But I must admit it was a lot of fun in the summer when we all went for a ride on Sunday afternoon with the top down, getting a suntan with the wind blowing our hair.

   Not only do you make people feel important when you ask for their ideas and recommendations about how to do something, but you also satisfy these desires as well:

   ✔ Recognition of efforts, reassurance of worth

✔ Approval and acceptance by others

✔ The feeling of belonging, being a member of the team

✔ The accomplishment of something worthwhile

✔ A sense of self-esteem, dignity, and self-respect

Marriage counselors have told me that the divorce rate is much lower with couples who use the participatory management technique. I've also learned from educational authorities that teenagers who come from families that practice this method in the home cause fewer disciplinary problems for their teachers. They also get along better with their fellow students.

Dr. Wanda Ellis, a clinical psychologist who specializes in family and marriage counseling, told me that a lot of husbands never tell their wives anything at all about their business, their work, or their plans for the future—even those that affect the entire family.

"They never give their wives a chance to make any sort of suggestion at all," Dr. Ellis said. "Yet they complain to me, saying their wives won't cooperate with them in saving money, economizing on household expenses, and so on. A lot of fathers say their children don't cooperate either, but they never ask them for their suggestions or ideas. They only order them around, telling them what to do or what not to do.

"I always recommend to my clients with family problems like this that the husband, wife, and children, too, sit down no less than once a month for a family conference. At this meeting, problems can be discussed, family goals established, and each person can be encouraged to offer suggestions and recommendations.

"I am always deeply gratified when people with seemingly insoluble problems are able to resolve them by adopting a family participative management plan. 'Impossible' situations are solved. The entire family gets along better. Everyone is much happier when each person is not dictated to but instead is asked for suggestions on solving family problems."

I recommend this method wholeheartedly. Although our own children are grown and gone now, the family conference, where we heard everybody's opinion and then voted on the problem, was our standard procedure for many years.

I always found that our children accepted parental authority more willingly, even when the decision went against them, when they had the chance to voice their own opinions and make suggestions before the final vote was taken.

I would also suggest that, as much as possible, you let your children make up their own rules of conduct to follow. I know that, just as employees do, they will obey their own rules and regulations more willingly than they will the ones the parents lay down for them. Of course, they still need your counsel and advice to help them make their decisions, for after all, you are older, more experienced, and generally wiser.

SOLUTIONS: HOW TO GET YOUR FAMILY TO DO WHAT YOU ASK THEM TO DO

If you want to *get* your family to do what you ask them to do, you must first *give* of yourself. Don't expect to get something from your family but give nothing in return just because they're your family.

If you want your spouse or your children to do something for you, then you must make the first move by doing something for them. Even in closely knit families that enjoy pleasant, harmonious relationships, the initial reaction to an order or a request is always *"What's in it for me?"* That's human nature and is to be expected. Perhaps that something you need to give them most of all is the *incentive* that will make them *want* to do as you desire.

I am reminded here of the fable of the old man who froze to death sitting in front of a stove with a huge pile of wood stacked up beside him because he was so stingy he didn't want to use it.

"Give me some heat," the old man said, stretching out his frozen hands toward the cold stove. "Then I'll give you some wood to burn."

But it is impossible to give nothing and get something in return. That happens only in fairy tales. So don't make the mistake of thinking you can give nothing and get something back. By the same token, it's impossible to give something and get nothing in return.

A petty, shortsighted person often refuses to give because he cannot see how or where he's going to profit by so doing. He gets nothing back because he gave nothing away. So you see, the maxim holds true even in this case. Just like the old man who froze to death in front of a stove with wood stacked up beside him, he got nothing back because that's exactly what he gave away: *nothing!*

This fable of the old man is not at all far-fetched. The same thing happens in real life. How many times have you picked up the newspaper to read where someone died in friendless *poverty* with thousands of dollars stored up in mattresses and cardboard boxes?

So remember that if you want your family to do what you want them to do, give them an incentive for doing it. Offer them a benefit when they do as you ask. Then they'll do as you ask. One of the biggest incentives you can use is to give them your love. When you do that, you'll get love back.

If you want to have your family do what you want them to do, it's a prerequisite that you establish a cheerful, happy atmosphere in your home. If you are a killjoy or have a critical attitude in your home, if you play favorites, or if you cause members of your family to feel constant fear and anxiety, you cannot possibly get the results that you want. Don't expect your spouse or your children to do what you want them to do if they are angry or filled with resentment toward you because of your dictatorial attitudes and actions.

Now here is one of the best ways you can give something away so you can get in return. First, let me say that to love and be loved are basic needs of every human being. And one of the best ways to express that love is to praise the other person for what he or she does.

When you use praise instead of criticism, you are fulfilling a basic human need. If you criticize, you're falling right into that old rut of trying to make your spouse over to fit your own standards, and that simply doesn't work. So always use praise instead of criticism to get results. It'll pay you rich dividends.

Do you have any idea how many of the basic needs and desires every person has that you can fulfill when you use praise? Let me list them for you so you can see for yourself how important it is to praise your spouse and your children rather than criticize them.

✔ Recognition of efforts; reassurance of worth

✔ Approval and acceptance

✔ A feeling of importance; ego-gratification

✔ The accomplishment or achievement of something worthwhile

✔ A sense of personal power

✔ Self-esteem; dignity; self-respect

✔ Love

✔ Emotional security

When you can fulfill eight of a person's basic needs and desires by using praise, then it makes good sense to do so. There is most definitely power in praise.

SOLUTIONS: HOW TO GUIDE YOUR CHILDREN WITHOUT EFFORT

Some months ago I sat listening to a group of psychiatrists, psychologists, and ministers discussing a fundamental question. All of these learned people were specialists in helping troubled people. The basic question they were discussing was what single factor was most important in their counseling. Was it insight? Experience? Training? Technique?

When the discussion was over, one single answer was agreed upon. It was that the counselor most likely to get results was the one who had mastered the art of listening, of paying attention to the troubled individual.

The reason for this is quite plain. Rich or poor, young or old, happy or unhappy, each of us yearns for attention. We want to be heard; we want to be listened to.

One psychiatrist, Dr. Craig Tyler, told us of a couple who had brought their fourteen-year-old boy to him for help. This boy had been a runaway. He had finally come home after being gone for nearly a year. Although his parents were glad to know that their prodigal son was all right, things were no better than before, according to what the young teenager said.

"Once I won the boy's confidence, it didn't take me long to find out what was really wrong," Dr. Tyler told us. "He told me that his parents didn't care about him. They never did anything together. He said his father never looked at him when he tried to talk with him and that all his mother ever did was nag him about the length of his hair, but she never listened to him either.

"I told those parents they had to learn to pay attention to their son. I told them that to PAY meant to part with something of value. In this case, that something was their time and their preoccupation with their own interests and pleasures.

"'Absence of attention is rejection,' I said to them. When you fail to pay attention to your child, you are rejecting him. *Rejection hurts. Attention heals. It's as simple as that.*"

This technique of paying attention to them will go a long way toward solving any disciplinary problems you're having with your children. I know, for I raised three of my own.

Many parents make the mistake of not paying attention to their children. They don't want to be bothered with them or their problems. But children need and want attention just as much as adults do, perhaps even more so.

It doesn't take a lot of extra effort to give your children that special attention they need so much. Ask them to play with you: perhaps a game of pool, table tennis, cards, chess, checkers, whatever you have available in your home.

My youngest son, Larry, and I used to battle it out with a cribbage board in front of the fireplace on many a stormy winter night when we lived in Missouri. In the summer time you had to wait in line to play ping-pong in our garage.

So learn to play with your children, pay attention to them. It'll improve all your family relationships. Your kids will learn to like you as well as love you. You'll not only be their parents but you'll also become their friends, and that's ever so important.

Praise is the best way I know of to show a person that you're paying full attention to him or her. Children respond to praise just as grownups do. If you want your son or daughter to get better grades in school, then praise them when they do well on a test or an assignment. If you criticize them for their grades, they'll go even lower. I guarantee that. I know that from personal experience.

I know that sometimes you must discipline your children, for as I told you, I raised three of my own. But discipline should be reasonable and firm, not brutal and severe. Parents in unhappy families don't realize this, but in a happy family there is seldom any reason for harsh discipline.

So give your children a happy home atmosphere, play with them, work with them, make them feel important by letting them take part in family affairs, and you'll find that most disciplinary problems disappear. Your children will do what you want them to do most of the time. And you'll be able to enjoy your children just as Mike Turner does.

"One summer a few years ago when Eddie was sixteen, he and I went on a month-long trip throughout Canada in a camper, just the two of us," Mike told me. "We did everything together as two buddies would. We took turns driving the pickup truck, cooking the meals, washing the dishes, and making the beds. Not once during that month did I tell him what to do. I treated him as a friend and as an equal.

"When we got back home, Eddie paid me a compliment that I will never forget. 'Dad, this has been the best time of my life,' he said to me. 'I'll always remember this trip, for I've learned that you're my friend as well as my father.'"

I must confess that there've been times when my sons were still home that I thought I was too busy to take time to play with them. I remember specifically one afternoon when I was busy writing another book in my home office.

My two sons, Bob and Larry, came in and said, "Dad, how about taking a break and going bowling with us." But I thought I was too busy to go so I declined. I've regretted that decision ever since! I don't remember what I was writing about, but I still remember turning down their invitation to bowl. And now my two sons are grown and gone and have children of their own to play with. And I'm still sitting here in my study writing another book!

Take every opportunity that comes your way to play with your kids and have fun with them. Don't make the mistake of turning down even a single one of their requests, as I so foolishly did. Your children are gone from the nest all too soon, as I have learned to my regret.

To conclude, let me say that I know you must give guidance and counsel to your children, but if you really want to enjoy them completely, drop that parent role as often as you can so you can play with them and be their friend as well as a father or a mother. This approach will bring you a wonderful new relationship with them.

SOLUTIONS: HOW TO CREATE A HAPPY FAMILY ATMOSPHERE

Each one of us possesses a power we all too often fail to use properly. That power is the *freedom of choice*. Many people choose poverty when they could choose to be rich. Some choose failure instead of success. Others choose to be afraid of life when all they need do is step out with courage and take what is rightfully theirs.

What you look to achieve in your family life is exactly the same. You have the power to choose the kind of home life that you want. You can choose one that is fun, filled with excitement, joy, and happiness. Or you can choose a home life that is constantly filled with anger, resentment, arguments, and bickering. It's all up to you.

I had an uncle whom I admired a great deal, Warren Roland. Uncle Warren and Aunt Opal were married for fifty-three years before he died. They were always wonderfully happy with each other. I never once heard a harsh word from either of them toward the other, nor did I ever see even an angry glance exchanged between them.

Just before I was married, Uncle Warren asked me to come by his place to chat for a while. "Will you accept a small bit of advice from your old uncle?" he asked. When I said that I would be only too glad to do so, here's what he told me:

"You can be happy in your marriage if you choose to be," he said. "That's what your Aunt Opal and I did when we were married many years ago. We chose to be happy. If you want your marriage to be successful, then I would recommend that you do the same. *Choose to be happy.* It's really just that simple if you don't complicate it.

"Sure, there'll be ups and downs. You won't be living on top of the mountain *every* day. No one can do that. You'll have some valleys in between that will be filled with sorrow, heartaches, and sadness. Your Aunt Opal and I have had those bad days, too. But we've weathered those storms because we made up our minds at the very beginning to be happy in our marriage no matter what happened.

"So if you choose to be happy in your marriage right here and now at the very start of your life together, and your new wife makes the same decision, then no matter what happens, your marriage will be a good one."

The value of my uncle's advice has not been dimmed by the passage of time. As far as I'm concerned, it's still good, so I'm passing it on to you. I've found it to be most valuable to me in my more than fifty years of married life.

Another small bit of advice about choosing happiness in your home life is this: Always be pleasant to your family no matter how rotten you might feel inside. There's no point in making your spouse and children miserable just because you're down in the dumps for some reason or other.

It is particularly important to develop the habit of pleasant, cheerful conversation when the family is all together. This is especially true at mealtimes. Do not upset everyone's digestion (including your own) by making the family meal a recitation of troubles, anxieties, fears, warnings, and accusations. Make every meal a joyful and festive occasion.

Let me give you another example, which I'm personally familiar with, of how important it is to choose to be happy in your marriage:

My beloved sister, Marjorie, and her husband, Ted, both had disastrous first marriages. In my sister's case, she never had the opportunity to choose to be happy, for her husband abused her both verbally and physically. I do not know all the details of Ted's first marriage; I never asked him about it and I never will.

But I do know that because of their very bad first marriages, both Marjorie and Ted chose to be happy together. And they were. I have visited them many times, and I have never seen two people more in love than they are.

I've heard it said that happy marriages are made in heaven and perhaps they are. But I also know that choosing to be happy has a lot to do with it, too.

Let me wrap this up by saying that even if you've been married a long time, it is never too late to make the choice to be happy with your spouse. No matter how bad things might seem to be at times, they'll always get better when you make that one simple decision. *Choose to be happy.*

SOLUTIONS: HOW TO CONDUCT A FAMILY "LOVE FEAST"

A unique method you can use to establish and maintain pleasant relationships in your marriage and your home life is to hold a family love feast.

Only two rules apply here: one, no criticism is allowed; two, only compliments are to be handed out. Here's an easy way to do that:

Gather your entire family in a comfortable setting, such as the family room, the den, or the living room. Soft, pleasant background music is permitted if it's turned down low, but no television and no other interruptions are allowed. Each person takes a turn being the subject while all the others tell him or her the good points they see and like about him or her. Let me give you some examples now:

"I love your awareness of natural beauty. You call my attention sometimes to a beautiful sunset or a gorgeous full moon and I think that's terrific, for then we can watch it together."

"I want to thank you for picking a gardenia and putting it on the table for me each morning. I do appreciate your loving thoughtfulness."

"I appreciate the way you always put the cap back on the toothpaste tube so it won't dry out."

"You're a warm, loving, and compassionate person, and I love you for that."

"Your smile and a cheerful 'Good morning' get me off to a good start each day. Thanks a lot!"

"Thanks a lot for not hanging your stockings on the shower rod. I really appreciate your thoughtfulness."

"You look fantastic in blue (or red or green)."

"I love to hear you sing, Mommy; you have such a beautiful voice."

"You really have a way with words, Dad. You explain everything so clearly I can understand it easily."

"You hit the ball better than anybody I know, Bob."

"You're an outstanding speller. I wish I had your talent for that, Teresa."

"I really love the cutting board you made for me in your shop class, Larry. Thanks a million."

There's no end to the good things you can say to each other in a family love feast. It helps the entire family to get along better, to understand each other, to appreciate each other more, to have fun with each other, and to look for the good qualities instead of the character defects in people.

Try using the same techniques with your friends and associates as well as with your family. Praise and kind words of appreciation for others can make irritable people warm and outgoing. Sad and despondent persons become confident and enthusiastic when they are treated to a love feast like this. So before you dismiss this technique as so much syrupy mush, give it a whirl. When you do, you'll quickly change your mind. You'll find it's a magic method that makes good sense.

MAKING YOUR MARRIAGE WORK

SOLUTIONS: HOW TO WORK MAGIC IN YOUR MARRIAGE

One of the real secrets to complete joy and happiness in your marriage is *accepting your partner exactly as he or she is.* Don't try to change your spouse and make him or her over into a second edition of yourself. Don't nag or criticize. You'll never change a person that way. Not only that, your marriage will suffer if you constantly nag, criticize, and find fault with your partner.

Take your own husband, for instance. Have you ever been able to change him very much through all your years of marriage by nagging and finding fault with him? You probably had good intentions. You felt you could make him over into the kind of person you thought he ought to be, but did you ever really succeed? I doubt it; I know my own wife never did!

Or if you're thinking of making your wife over to fit your own specifications by using criticism, forget it. I failed at that one, too. I haven't been able to change my wife one bit through all these years. She's still the same woman that I married. But I'm glad I failed in this. I realize now that I couldn't have improved on her at all.

233

This is a most valuable point for you to remember. *The only person you can ever really change in life is you—no one else!* So accept your marriage partner just as he or she is. You'll be much happier when you do.

As an example, let me tell you about an extreme case. I once knew a woman whose husband had a real problem and she desperately wanted to change him. Mrs. K. had a family of five children and a husband who'd been drunk and out of work for nearly all of their twenty-five years of marriage. She had supported the family most of that time herself by working in a department store.

Every possible treatment and approach that had been tried to solve her husband's alcoholism had failed. For religious reasons, Mrs. K. did not want to divorce her husband, but at the same time, she simply could not accept him the way he was. And since she was unable to change him, her misery and despair became deeper and deeper.

Then one day she made the most important discovery of her entire married life. "There is absolutely nothing I can do to change Dan or solve his drinking problem," she told herself. "But that is his problem, not mine. I'm powerless to change him or to solve his problem for him. I cannot live his life for him. He is a sick man, an alcoholic, and I am going to give up the idea right now that I can ever get him to stop drinking. From now on, I am not going to torture myself with his problem any longer. I am going to accept things exactly the way they are.

"I will take care of him, of course, for he is my husband, and I still love him in spite of everything. But I am going to quit trying to change him. I am going to accept him just as he is and do whatever I can to make my own life and the lives of my children as happy as possible under these circumstances."

Mrs. K. was finally admitting to herself that she was powerless to change her husband. Her new view of the situation worked wonders for both herself and her children. It did not stop her husband from drinking; only he could do that. But in spite of his drinking problem, Mrs. K. and her children all began to live comparatively normal and happy lives again.

Realizing that you cannot change your husband or your wife— even in matters far less significant than alcoholism—can help you the same way. In fact, you'll never be able to achieve total joy and happiness in your marriage until you do accept your spouse exactly as he or she is.

SOLUTIONS: HOW TO HELP YOUR SPOUSE SUCCEED

The techniques I'll give you here will work for either spouse in a marriage.

But first let me tell you about Barbara T. Barbara's marriage of more than twenty years seemed headed for the divorce courts. She called me one day in tearful desperation to see if I could somehow help her.

"I don't know what to do," she said. "Bill just doesn't seem satisfied with me any more no matter what I do. In fact, it seems that everything I do is wrong. He doesn't like the way I keep house, the meals I cook, the way I dress; and says I'm cold in bed. He's constantly picking at me and criticizing what I do.

"We went to see a marriage counselor, but that didn't help at all. Can you do anything for us, Jim? I don't like to bother you, but you're one of my closest friends, and I thought with your experience in applied psychology and being a writer and all, you could think of something that could help us. I really do love Bill and I can't bear the thought of losing him. Then there are the children to consider, too."

What I told Barbara helped her to save her marriage. When she used the techniques I told her about and put them to work, her marital problems vanished into thin air. Whether you're having trouble in your marriage or not, I'm sure they can help you improve your own marital relationships, too. Here's what they are.

1. *Make your spouse the most important person in your life*. How can you do this? Well, the first thing to do is simply to tell yourself and mean it that your spouse *is* the most important person in your life. Do this and you won't have to pretend. Your attitude will get across to him or her without your even trying.

Not only that, you won't have to use gimmicks and tricks to make this technique work. Your relations with your mate will be on an honest and sincere basis. As you think so shall you believe, and as you believe, so shall it be. Act as if it were true, and it will be true. Remember what I've said before, you become what you think about.

2. *Pay close attention to everything she says and does*. This is one of the best ways of making her the most important person in your life. One of the most common complaints of both wives and husbands is this: "He (or she) never notices me, never pays any attention to me, takes me for granted, treats me like an old shoe."

Does your wife have a new hairdo? Tell her how beautiful it makes her look. Is she wearing a new dress? Compliment her on her wise choice. Thank her for the wonderful dinner.

I once heard of a wife who was so tired of not receiving any attention from her husband that she met him at the front door when he came home from work wearing nothing but a tiny kitchen apron that revealed everything and left nothing to the imagination. You can bet that her husband paid very close attention to her from then on. "What if I'd been a delivery man?" he said.

Your wife might not need to go that far to get your attention, but just to play it safe, I recommend that you give her your full, wholehearted attention at all times. It'll pay you tremendous dividends.

3. *Always praise; never criticize*. As I mentioned earlier, praise is one of the best ways you can express your love for the other person. Praise your spouse and make him or her feel important. Just say, "I'm so proud of you." He'll almost turn cartwheels to make you feel even prouder of him.

You can help your spouse become more successful by the simple act of praising him for what he does. Praise builds his self-confidence. Criticism destroys it. Here's what I mean:

Armond L., president of a huge corporation employing several thousand employees, told me that many big businessmen and corporation executives want to find out something about a man's wife before they promote him to a top-level position of responsibility.

"We are more interested in whether she gives her husband a feeling of confidence in himself than we are in her good looks and social acceptability," Armond says.

"You see, if she accepts her husband without criticism, if she gives him the feeling that she is pleased with him, and if she praises him in every way possible, it's like getting a shot in the arm every time he comes home. His wife's praise sends him off each morning filled with the self-confidence that he can lick any problem that comes his way. And that's the kind of person we need in our top executive slots."

SOLUTIONS: HOW TO CORRECT YOUR SPOUSE'S BAD HABITS

When a couple is first married, they are completely blind to each other's faults. They're still too much in love to pay any attention to the other person's bad habits. But after the honeymoon is over and they realize there are some adjustments that have to be made, there can be a tendency to find fault and criticize each other. Then it is all too easy for love to fly out the window.

But this doesn't have to happen. Here are some techniques that you can use to gain loving consideration from each other without destroying your happy relationship.

SITUATION: Husband always leaves the cap off the toothpaste tube.

WIFE'S WRONG REACTION: For heaven's sake, when will you ever learn to put the cap back on the toothpaste tube? I'm sick and tired of trying to get the toothpaste out of the tube when it's all dried up. If you can't put the top back on, then get your own toothpaste!

WIFE'S CORRECT REACTION: Darling, would you mind putting the cap back on the toothpaste tube when you finish using it so it won't dry up? I'd sure appreciate it if you would do that. Thanks a lot, sweetheart, for being so thoughtful.

SITUATION: Wife hangs her stockings over the shower rod to dry and leaves her cosmetics scattered all over the bathroom counter.

HUSBAND'S WRONG REACTION: Why the devil do you always hang your stockings on the shower rod? Can't you find someplace else to dry them? I can't take a shower when they're in my way. And I need a broom to clean up your mess on the bathroom counter. I've never seen so much junk in all my life. Do you need all that to put your face on in the morning? I can't even find a clean place to shave and wash up.

HUSBAND'S CORRECT REACTION: Honey, I'd really appreciate it if you didn't hang your stockings over the shower rod until after I take my shower. Or if you hang them up at night, could you please take them down each morning before I go in to shower? I don't want to get them wet or make you wash them all over again. And honey, could you put away your makeup when you've finished putting it on? I don't want to spill any soap or water or shaving cream on your things while I'm getting cleaned up and ready to go to work. Thanks! I love you.

SITUATION: Husband throws his dirty clothes in a corner, tosses his pants over the arm of the closest chair, and drops his shoes when he comes in the front door.

WIFE'S WRONG REACTION: I'd swear your mother raised a pig instead of a son. If you think I'm going to follow you around the house picking up after you, you're crazy. I'm sick and tired of your stupid, filthy, lazy habits!

WIFE'S CORRECT REACTION: Honey, I'd appreciate it if you'd put your dirty things in the clothes hamper and hang your trousers up on a hanger so they won't get so wrinkled. I just don't have the time to press your pants every day. And this morning I nearly fell over your shoes in the hallway when I went out to get the morning paper for you. Darling, I can't hold down a job and keep a clean house, too, unless you help me. Would you please do that? Thanks, dear.

I could go on and on with other examples like these, but these three should be enough to show you how to solve those small irritating problems with courtesy and kindness instead of nagging and criticism. If you do that, you'll be able to keep the fires of love and romance burning all your life and have a marriage like the kind in fairy tales.

INDEX